The Blue Expanse
Selected poems

by

Anwar Salman

Translated and edited by

Nizar Sartawi

inner child press, ltd.

Credits

Author
Anwar Salman

Editor
Nizar Sartawi

Translator
Nizar Sartawi

Cover Design
Inner Child Press, ltd.

General Information

The Blue Expanse
Anwar Salman
Translated by Nizar Sartawi

1st Edition : 2018

This Publishing is protected under Copyright Law as a "Collection". All rights for all submissions are retained by the Individual Artist and/or Author. No part of this Publishing may be Reproduced, Transferred in any manner without the prior **WRITTEN CONSENT** of the "Material Owner" or its Representative Inner Child Press. Any such violation infringes upon the Creative and Intellectual Property of the Owner pursuant to International and Federal Copyright Law. Any queries pertaining to this "Collection" should be addressed to Publisher of Record.

Publisher Information
1st Edition : Inner Child Press :
innerchildpress@gmail.com
www.innerchildpress.com

This Collection is protected under U.S. and International Copyright Laws

Copyright: Arabic text of poems © 2018 : Anwar Salman
English text of poems © 2018 : Nizar Sartawi

ISBN-13 : 978-1970020465 (inner child press, ltd.)
ISBN-10 : 1970020466

$ 16.95

Dedication

This Book is dedicated to

the soul of Lebanese poet

Anwar Salman

Table of Contents

Acknowledgements   11
Preface   13
Introduction   17

The Poetry   27

From To Her   29

O Moon   30
We Are Done   32
A Letter   34
A Pair Of Lips   38
Her Hair   40
Spring   44
You No Longer Remember…   48
Laugh   50

From Colored Cards For An Age With No Festive Days   53

A Bouquet Of Flowers For Her Birthday   54
Interval   56
Said The Storyteller   58
On The Margin Of Dialogue   60
Wounds   62
The Train   64
The Christ Of The Nation   66

Table of Contents...*continued*

A Question	68
A Face For Another Homeland	70
Fog	72
The Blue Expanse	74
These	76
Something Out Of Nothing	78
I Don't Want An Apology	80
The Beauty Of Beauties	82
Sailing	84

From I Search In Your Eyes For A Homeland — 87

Little Details	88
The Runaway Date	90
The Last Leaf	92
Candles That Give No Light	94
Sunset	96
Your Eyes Are Summer Nights	98
Dreams On The Rhone	100
A Sailor	102
A More Beautiful Morrow	104
A Piece From Heaven	106
Prime Of Life	108
Giving	110
The Anthem Of Roses And The Sun	112
A Procession	114
A Cloudy Sky	116

Table of Contents ... *continued*

From The Poem Is An Impossible Woman   119

    A Green Quill   120
    A Song For A Passer-By   122
    A Prayer Outside The Church   124
    A Telephone Call   126
    Childhood   128
    Silent Music   130
    Ink On Paper   132
    A Play   134
    Custody   136
    A Traveler   138
    The Bird Of Ink   140
    Composition   142
    Waiting For A Visa   144

From Mirrors For Runaway Dreams   147

    Traveling With The Sail Of The Sun   148
    Thunder And Lightning   150
    Departure   152
    The Path Of Poetry   154
    A Wound And A Rose   156
    With Light… Upon The Homeland Soil   158
    Lamps   160
    Modernism   162
    Greater Than All Languages   164

Table of Contents...*continued*

A Rose Inside A Book	166
Your Eyes And I	168
Letters From The Age Of Poetry	170
Man And Earth	172
Words Never To Be Forgotten	174

Epilogue   177

About the Author	179
About the Translator	183
What Critics Said About Anwar Salman	185
Notes	189

Acknowledgments

First I praise God for His endless blessings.

I would like to thank all those people who have helped me in completing this work. I thank Zulfa Sartawi, my wife and soul-mate, who has always stood by me and supported me with her patience and steadfastness.

I bow with deep respect and gratitude before my friend poet and translator Ute Margaret Saine, who has not only proofread this book so meticulously, but also has written an exceptional introduction for it.

I would like to express my deep gratitude to my friend Nashaat Salman for reading my translation word for word and for his insightful suggestions.

And last but not least, I would like to express my great appreciation of the tremendous support that my friend, poet William S. Peters Sr., CEO, Inner Child Press has blessed me with.

Preface

In undertaking the translation of the poems included in *The Blue Expanse,* my main objective was to introduce Anwar Salman, a Lebanese renowned poet, to the English-speaking readers. Salman's poetic career started in 1956, when the young poet, still a high school student, won Maroun Aboud Prize for Poetry; and it came to an end in an unfortunate car accident on April 20, 2016. During these six decades, Salman's poetry was read with passion by so many Arab poetry enthusiasts in Lebanon and other Arab countries. Moreover, many of his poems were set to melody and sung by famous Arab singers, and some of these poems won prestigious prizes in major Arab song festivals.

For many critics Salman is one of the best Arab lyric modern poets. Lyricism of course is not a literary movement. Rather, it is a broad term that can be applied to a spectrum of creative arts, including, music, painting, dance, film, and even architecture. In poetry, in particular, the term lyricism has been widely used to describe poetry belonging to different literary ages and different regions, as well as diverse poetry schools.

Lyric poetry is generally characterized by its privity, tendency to be personal, emotional intensity, and musical quality; and these attributes can be clearly seen in Salman's poetry. Salman was never inclined to write long poems. Most of his poems are short or even very short, ranging between a few lines and four or five pages. In fact, of all the 70 poems included in *The Blue Expanse*, and they are fairly representative of his poetry, only three exceed one page.

Nor is the emotional aspect lacking in these poems. Whether courting a woman, expressing his love for his homeland, commenting on a national event, embarking on a poetic or spiritual journey, or giving voice to his discontent with the political upheavals that his country witnessed, Salman does not repress his feelings. Regardless of the theme he treats, he is far from taking a detached attitude; there is always a personal tone that rings loud in his poetry.

With regard to musicality, which is mainly about rhythm and rhyme, but is also concerned with other aural elements, Salman did not consistently conform to classical Arabic rules of prosody. Like many of his contemporaries, he experimented with new forms that deviated from the unswerving regularity of old patterns, employing a more open style in which the rhythm, or metrical scheme, is maintained without adhering to the length of the line, i.e., using a fixed number of feet for all the lines of the poem. Likewise, he did not stick to the single-rhyme pattern, i.e. employing the same rhyme for the whole poem regardless of its length.

More significantly, however, Salman, like all great poets, uses a simple language that flows smoothly like a quiet river – a language which is laden with vivid imagery and metaphor, giving words fresh meanings. Language for him is a vehicle through which he expresses his noble sentiments: his love for life, for people, for his country, and for beauty.

In this sense, Salman, who has been recognized as one the icons of modern Arabic poetry, was truly *modern*. He strongly believed in the necessity for change, but he could never reconcile himself with the more radical trends which called for adopting a totally liberal style in which not only rhythm and rhyme are abandoned, but language itself becomes distorted, losing its essence and sense of purpose, and is consequently deprived of its beauty. "We have forgotten," he wrote bitterly,

> how poetry was written on our sky-colored pages…!
> … In the congestion of languages which changed even the color of our eyes... words in our notebooks no longer have warmth or fragrance, as though they were flowers carved from stone, that can neither be written nor spoken…!" ("Modernism," *The Blue Expanse*).

Perhaps this confirms that Salman came close to creating a new theory of poetry, as one critic suggested.

Nevertheless, Salman, like most modern and contemporary Arab poets, has not been translated into English, or any other language. Unfortunately, few translators have made the effort to do that, possibly because literary translators, often discouraged by the challenges involved in translating from their mother tongue to a foreign language, are generally advised to translate only into their own language since their mastery of the second language and knowledge of the culture it represents can rarely be equal to that of their native language and culture. Or maybe they are intimidated by the very idea of translating poetry, owing to the view that poetry does not lend itself to translation.

My own conviction is that Salman and many other important poets in the Arab region should be heard by the world. And this cannot happen without translating their works. For me, however, this endeavor implies more than just introducing a significant Arabic poetic voice to the English-speaking world. I have been driven by a deep affinity within my soul that connected me with Anwar Salman. By reading and translating his poems, I pay tribute to a poet who has inspired me as well as hundreds of poets and millions of poetry lovers.

Nizar Sartawi

Introduction

"Traveling to the gate of the absolute": The Poetry of Anwar Salman

Lebanon is by tradition a country of many poets, one of the most recent being Anwar Salman, revealed to us here in a book of excellent translations by the Palestinian poet and writer Nizar Sartawi. This book, *The Blue Expanse,* gathers translated selections from several substantive books of poems Anwar Salman has previously published in Arabic, since 1959 – up and including the 2017 collection *Mirrors For Runaway Dreams* – and so may be considered a summa of Salman's lyrical work in English. The poet Anwar Salman is not unknown in these parts; one of his poems, "I Don't Want an Apology", was chosen as the best poem at the Carthage Poetry Festival in Tunisia, in 1994. In the following, I will attempt to let the poet's words speak for themselves as much as possible.

And impressive it is, this book. At the outset, Anwar Salman characterizes himself, speaking from among the poles of his concerns, his love for country and his love for love and beauty:

I'm a lovesick wanderer
in the horizon of song
upon the chest of beauty
I lay my head to rest.

"[I]n the horizon of song/upon the chest of beauty"—we immediately grasp the poetic power that lies in such pithy one-liners as this one. The poet is courageous and encouraged to perform his task of writing:

I light the candles of alphabets around me
and go on
with a thousand colors in my feather,

returning the pen he writes with to the goose feather it came from, which permits poetic flight. And in the poem "Spring", allied with the spring season, such words become the epitome of poetic breath and intuition:

Magic is my expanse
Inspiration surrounds me
shades me
and flutters with a smile.

In this book, Salman slowly builds up the composition of a complex ode to his country. He addresses his friends and readers: "I will be content if one day it is said: that at the time of tyranny which set the homeland on fire… I hid my country… a rose inside a book!" In the poem "Said The Storyteller", the poet resumes in the vein of the ancient storyteller tradition:

I have a country
about whom we've been told
the sweetest tales.
A wall of mountains she is…

And one of the distinguishing qualities of Lebanon is precisely its poetry, its poetic speech and diction. This is how Anwar Salman describes it, in a hymn addressed to his home country:

My country…
O lavender fragrance
My country…
my pasture, my world of passion

My country…
my bride of poetry
O Lebanon.

There is a distinctly erotic note in the evocation of his home country, there is a love that contaminates the feeling of home and childhood that Lebanon stands for in the poet's conscience:

And there they were
your face… your voice…
your heart
O Lebanon!

And in "The Prime of Life", the poet clearly expresses this overwhelming feeling of closeness and affection:

My homeland is love…
Is there a heart
that has a sweeter date
or a lovelier bosom?

But the identity of poetry and home country has been badly shaken and compromised in recent history. There is a dark cloud endangering the poetry of the land, the poetic land:

But when the storyteller
concludes his tales
and we go to bed,
we glimpse a tear in the eye of the messages!
and see the hands that raise the flags of peace
open fire on
all the words!

In the poem "Custody", Anwar Salman ascribes this to a fatal tendency in human beings, or generic "man": "Whenever indulging in sins/he ascribes them to heaven." Events are out of hand, have become incomprehensible and uncontrollable, things suddenly fall apart today that yesterday were still intact, and people become lonely with sadness, which the poet resents and expresses as an overwhelming, incomprehensible menace: "You pass as a broken sword on my eyelids, though yesterday you were a hand that picked the moon…!" And the poet finishes with the anguished cry: "Who is it who loves to travel upon your wounds?"

Here,
the tragedy in history takes
the shape
of a train

from which the smoke of night ascends
in the plains
of the day

Here the frequent image of travel comes to the fore, which in some poems, such as "Waiting for a Visa", carries a distinctly hopeful, utopian note:

How beautiful it would be

*If the Earth were
for all people
a free homeland with no restrictions!*

The poet has to acknowledge that not all people in his country are straight, but rather recognizes them as devious in their duplicity: "They carried pencils for a cause:/They rejected creativity in all literary/ages." And imploringly, in a country and region of many wars, the poet Anwar Salman conjures up a Lebanon that would become a "world of peace" and "love":

*My homeland is love…
Is there a heart
that has
a sweeter date
or a lovelier bosom?*

And at the end of the moving poem with the telling title "A Face for Another Homeland", the poet confesses and avers:

*Here is a tear
for your morning from a poet.
Peace be upon you, my homeland.*

The poet is the dreamer; he is a "lunatic" living under the benign light of the moon. In the poem "Dreams on the Rhône", which includes a trip to Geneva and Lac Léman, he finds the spirits of other world poets who went before him, in their consoling as much as disquieting presence:

*On the surface of the water
Byron's hymns
and Rimbaud's dreams*

*looked
like wounds!*

But the poet survives and subsists on the moon, as the poem titled "O Moon" suggests:

*How many dates with you do I have...?
Do stop by the Moon Path*

*My home is there
Drop by
Mine you are, all that I wish for
Mine you are... O moon.*

Salman's poetic mission is complicated and compromised by the warring that tears up his homeland, and he laments, filled with regrets:

*My visions lead me away as if I were
traveling to the gate of the absolute, so it seems!*

*If I return... I'll have a horizon in my hands
And if I meet my end... I'll drown in dreams*

But the poet's task becomes increasingly complicated. He complains: "I'm all alone/An inkwell lying on my tablelike a question!" Bad news, or no news break his spirit, perplexing him into confusion and pushing him into stagnation, as a writer:

*I try to break... my silence
by writing.
My lip:
no roses dwell in its blood*

no visions
where oases glow amidst the gloom of thoughts!
I have no choice but to break the pencils.
And thus the dialogue
comes to an end.

On the principal topic of love, the poet has this to say, speaking for himself. Love as an event, and soon a memory, will be forever alive:

Our drunken kisses
beside the brook... were blown
by the fragrance
to the mountainside... to the path of grapevines.

The poet is a searcher on a quest, his goal is to search for beauty and love through the contemplation of his loved one:

Beauty of beauties, in your face
I'm searching for a glorious sun
hidden away by the scarf of clouds.

I'm searching for a lost summer star...
that has escaped from the home of stars

In fact, the quest for poetry and the quest for love become one and the same, as the poet marshals his words in ever new poems. The title of his 2008 book is precisely *The Poem Is An Impossible Woman*. And so he gives the loved one "a bouquet of words." But in some role poems, the poet even adopts the female voice; he lets the woman speak, or becomes her mouthpiece, her secretary:

*The thoughts are hers
and mine the script,
the scent,
the dewy lip.*

In his verses, a poetic dialogue between the poet and his beloved is established, emanating from "[h]er mouth [which] was a blossoming call":

*A pair of lips for me
one I reproach
the other reproaches me...*

The poet's inspirations stall: "A closed notebook/in which a poem/came to a halt at the first line!" But the beloved, doing what all beloveds do, inspires by mere presence:

*And then you come in
like a star
from the window of imagination
and in my alphabets you leave
for love
the most beautiful thing that beauty can ever say!*

Holding the loved one is when a human life is allowed to travel to the confines of the absolute:

*Who are you?
The magic in your eyes
fulfills a wish in my life
As though you have come from a moon
or from a golden morning star!
from a land where the sun of love
embraces the face of liberty.*

Though on the horizon, there always remains the danger of falling out of love. In "The Runaway Date", the poet observes:

The sky of love went cloudy,
those stars
faded away; our faces were both lost.

And he adds despondently, in "The Last Leaf":

We planted the dream…
in the balconies of the sun
but we lost all its paths.
…
Nothing has been left…
of our story
save burnt paper.

But the old dreams return; at one point the poet exclaims nostalgically about an old flame: "That childhood/of love…/How sweet it was!" And in the role poem "Her hair--the woman's poem", the woman finally speaks for herself:

My soul I give for you… O dark-skinned
Your opinion I hold dear
I'll loosen my hair
so that when you see me
you'll love me…
love me
even more…!

This memorable collection of poems is fueled by love and a fervent desire for peace in the Middle East. The poet says "The sun of wounds will never set/for from the wound the impossible is born." But at the same time, we can be sure of it; "the sun of words will never set" either, in this moving, magical poetic collection by Anwar Salman. I end with a poem that exemplifies the mysterious and felicitous nexus between love, poetry and life:

A Green Quill

You are my star
Keep my night illuminated
when
my days are transformed into travel.
I write with light,
My pages are a sky
that has drunk
the seasons
from the color of your eyes
I've always carried the sun with me,
while...
painting an impossible dream
I'd never loved night
until
you became the green quill
and lovely poetry.

Margaret Saine [1]

The Blue Expanse

The Poetry

Anwar Salman

Anwar Salman

Selections From

To Her
(1959)

مختارات من ديوان

إليها
(1959)

O Moon

One April evening… on the village path… this beautiful story-song came to pass

How many dates with you do I have…?
Do stop by the Moon Path
My home is there
Drop by
Mine you are, all that I wish for
Mine you are… O moon

~ ~ ~ ~

There we were, were not the stars aware?
Our drunken kisses
beside the brook… were blown
by the fragrance
to the mountainside… to the path of grapevines
and upon your eyelids there were songs
a fanciful dream…
Speak O my sweetheart
I do not care… Let lasses gossip
I do not care… Let people talk
About my date
about the color of my dream tomorrow
wonderful tales will be told

~ ~ ~ ~

I love you…
you, who stand in high esteem
Take from my hand
bouquets of flowers
O you, my dreams of tomorrow
O you, my moon…!

يا قمر

في إحدى عشيات نيسان... على دروب القرية... كانت هذه الاغنية الجميلة:

كمْ موعدٍ لي في لقاكُ...
عرّجْ على درب القمرْ
بيتي هناكَ
مرَّ بنا..
لي أنتَ يا كلَّ المنى
لي... يا قمرْ

~ ~ ~ ~

كنّا، ألمْ تذرِ بنا كلُّ النجومْ
قُبلاتنا عندَ الغديرْ
سكرى.. يُطيّرها العبيرْ
في السفحِ.. في درب الكرومْ
وعلى جفونكَ أغنياتْ
حلمٌ غريبْ..
قلْ يا حبيبْ
ما همَّني.. تحكي البناتْ
ما همَّني.. عنّي يُقالْ
عن موعدي،
عن لون حلمٍ في غدي
تُروى حكاياتُ الجمالْ

~ ~ ~ ~

أهواكَ..
يا طيّب الذِّكرْ
خُذْ من أضاميم الزَهرْ
خُذْ من يدي
يا كلَّ أحلامِ الغدِ
يا... يا قمرْ..!

We Are Done

Say: We're done…
and the promise is over
Tell me…
Anything left for love…?

In our eyes love is but foolish
images…
with which no pledge could be fulfilled

Our tale… has died…
Eyelids allure
no more…
nor lips… nor arms

This pleasant emptiness
has buried us…
as if the dreams of love were sleepless nights
What value do our longings have if they
pass through our fancies when we on purpose shun each
other

O beautiful lady…
all our chats were just a bunch of lies…
Gentle reproaches
longings… and promises were all lies too

Say we're done…
Our love is just a wreckage…
on whose relics glory cries

انتهينا

قولي: انتهينا..
وانقضى الوعدُ..
قولي..
أشيءٌ للهوى بعدُ..؟

الحبّ في أحداقنا صُوَرٌ
بلهاءُ..
لا يزهو لها عهدُ

ماتتْ.. حكايتنا..
فلا هُدُبٌ..
تغوى..ولا شفةٌ.. ولا زندُ

هذا الفراغ الحُلْوُ
يدفعنا..
فكأنّ أحلام الهوى سُهْدُ

ما قيمةُ الأشواقِ إن عبرتْ
بخيالنا وجفاؤنا قصدُ

حسناءُ..
كل حديثنا.. كذبٌ..
وعتابُنا..
والشوق.. والوعدُ

قولي انتهينا..
حبّنا طَلَلٌ..
يبكي على أنقاض المَجدُ

A Letter

The thoughts are hers
and mine the script,
the scent,
the dewy lip,

the beauty of my date with her,
and some news
that the evening goes wild about

These lines are well-wrought
leafy…
vivid

Her evening,
akin to roses, covers me
with scents

She wrote me a gentle reproach
and the whole night
was filled with tender melodies

Anonymous she was
Her signature was curved
lavishly
and fondly

The cherry-like smiling lips
have left in the letter
a present for me

~ ~ ~ ~

This is a phantom akin to spring
embracing me
This is a lass

رسالة

أفكارُها،
والخطّ لي
والطيبُ،
والشفةُ النديّةْ

وجمالُ موعدها،
وأخبارٌ
تجنُّ بها العشيّةْ

هذي سطورٌ حلوة التنسيقِ
مورقةٌ..
غنيّةْ

ومساؤها،
كالورودِ يغمرني،
بأطيابٍ شهيّةْ

كتبتْ تعاتبني..
فكلّ الليل،
أنغامٌ طريّةْ

مجهولةٌ،
إمضاؤها يلتفُّ
في ترفٍ
وغيّةْ

والمبسمُ الكرزيّ
يتركُ في الرسالةِ
لي هديّةْ
~ ~ ~ ~
هذا خيالٌ كالربيع
يضمّني..
هذي صبيّةْ

Her fragrant breeze
ornamented sleeve
lily-like arm

and a magic letter
inscribed with the pen
of a prophetess

A heart
and breaths
and eyelids that I almost touched –
and they were so yielding

and a black tassel
inviting me
and sending me greetings

ربَّاها..
والكمّ المزركشُ
والذراعُ الزنبقيَّهْ

ورسالةٌ مسحورةٌ
كتبتْ بأقلامٍ
نبيَّهْ

قلبٌ..
وأنفاسٌ،
وهُدْبٌ كدتُ ألمسها
رضيَّهْ

وجديلةٌ سوداءُ
تدعوني،
وتبعثُ لي تحيَّهْ

A Pair Of Lips

A mouth
going mad with desire
suffering for a kiss

A lip that has some poetry
in my heart
Her wishes all will granted be

A pair of lips…!
unmatched by tulips…!
or fresh lilies

Two rubies…
that dew
would be amazed
to come across

A pair of lips…!
O how longings tire my bosom
with their wailing

A pair of lips for me
one I reproach
the other reproaches me

شفتان

ثغرٌ..
يجنّ، ويرغبُ
وبقبلةٍ يتعذّبُ

شفةٌ لها في خاطري
شِعرٌ..
لها ما تطلبُ

شفتان..!
ما التوليبُ.. ما...!
ما الزنبقُ المسترطبُ

ياقوتتانِ..
إذا التقى بهما الندى
يستغربُ

شفتان..!
للأشواقِ في صدري
نُواحٌ مُتعِبُ

شفتان لي..
شفةٌ أعاتِبها،
وأخرى تعتبُ.

Her Hair

Your opinion I hold dear
I'll undo this lazy knot
loosen my hair
and let it down on my shoulders
so that when you see me
you'll tell me that I'm comeliest this way

~ ~ ~ ~

Tomorrow my hair will be in the prettiest style
falling freely on my blue dress
 I'll look more alluring than the whole world…
younger than lilies…
with pride I'll wear it…
 fall in love…
 walk as with a waterfall of scents
wipe it with my eyelids
bring it close to my face… whisper to it…
fold it… embrace it… coddle it

My hair
with its new look
my hair tomorrow in the prettiest style
the loveliest present on my first date

~ ~ ~ ~

By Lord, O poet!
My hair in its rebellious look
won't you sing for it…?
What presents will you have for it…?
Will you bring perfume… images
anemones from the farthest islands
ribbons from the aperture of the moon?

شعرُها

لي رأيكَ الاغلى
سأفكّ هذي العقدة الكسلى
شعري سأرخيهِ..
مُلقى على كتفي سأبقيهِ..
حتى إذا شاهدتني فيه..
أخبرتني أنّي به أحلى

~ ~ ~ ~

شعري غداً في شكله الأجملْ
مُرخى على فستانيَ الأزرقْ
أبدو به أغوى من الدنيا..
أصبى من الزنبقْ..
أزهو به..
أهوى به.. أعشقْ
أمشي به شلّالَ أطيابِ
أفديهِ، أمسحُهُ بأهدابي
أدنيهِ من وجهي.. أناجيهِ..
أطويه.. أغمرُهُ.. أداريهِ
شعري أنا..
شعري بما فيهِ
شعري غداً في شكلهِ الاجملْ
أحلى هدايا الموعد الأولْ

~ ~ ~ ~

باللهِ يا شاعرْ
شعري غداً في شكله الثائرْ
هلاَّ تُغنّيه..
ماذا ستُهديهِ..؟
أتجيئُهُ بالعطر.. بالصُوَرِ
بشقائق من أبعدِ الجزرِ
بشرائطٍ من كُوّةِ القمرِ

Anwar Salman

Tell me…
Will you love me for it…?

~ ~ ~ ~

My soul I give for you… O dark-skinned
Your opinion I hold dear
I'll loosen my hair
so that when you see me
you'll love me…
love me
even more…!!

قلْ لي..
أسوْفَ تحبّني فيه..؟

~ ~ ~ ~

أفديكَ.. يا أسمرْ
لي رأيكَ الأغْلى
شعري سأرخيهِ
حتى إذا شاهدتني فيهِ
أحببتني..
أحببتني..
أكثرْ..!!

Spring

My country…
O lavender fragrance
My country…
my pasture, my world of passion

My country…
my bride of poetry
O Lebanon
O world of peace

O how poems have been recited
upon your lips…
how shrines of poetry have been raised upon your land

Is it a dream in your eyelids
or a ghost
alluring me with a passionate lover's smile?

~ ~ ~ ~

I'm a lovesick wanderer
in the horizon of song
upon the chest of beauty
I lay my head to rest

In the wave of perfume I dart
and call on the brides
of love

Violets court me
along my paths
and the planets run ahead of me

ربيع

بلادي..
يا عبيراً من خزامِ
بلادي..
مرتعي، ودُنا هيامي

بلادي..
يا عروس الشعر عندي
ويا لبنانُ
يا دنيا السلامِ

على فمكَ القصائدُ
كم ترامتْ..
وكم للشّعرِ فوقك من مقامِ

وحلمٌ في جفونك..
أم خيالٌ
يراودني.. ببسمة مستهامِ

~ ~ ~ ~

أنا هيمان..
في أفق التغنّي
على صدرِ الجمالِ
أريحُ هامي..

أسوح بموجةِ العطر انطلاقاً
واستدعي العرائس
من غرامِ

يغازلني البنفسج
في دروبي..
وتنطلقُ الكواكبُ من أمامي

Anwar Salman

The horizon expands freely
in my eyelids
and dreams have their share of my wine

Magic is my expanse
Inspiration surrounds me
shades me
and flutters with a smile

In my homeland I am… the beauty of my poetry
is a spring
of my fascination

فللأفقِ انعتاقٌ
في جفوني
وللأحلامِ جزءٌ من مُدامي

مداي السحرُ..
والألهام حولي..
يظلّلُني
ويخفقُ.. بابتسامِ

أنا في موطني.. وجَمال شعري
ربيعٌ في رياضه..
من هيامي

You No Longer Remember…

The poet modified the original text and it was sung by Fayza Ahmed, a famous Syrian-Egyptian singer.

You no longer remember our love vows
how we fared and how was our love

O beloved you've forgotten the days of my love
and promises that tenderly longed for you

Our home is a stranger with flying paths?
inquiring of the night and forenoon about our tryst

We built a realm of fidelity for love
but our hands treated love unkindly

Our love… our love is but a summer cloud
a mirage where our steps have been rushing

There we tasted bitterness and cruelty
and had our share of its bitterness

O beloved I asked the nights about you
as the nights resounded our echo

Come back at dawn smiling for wishes
Love has none O beloved save ourselves

لم تعد ذاكراً

قام الشاعر بتعديل نصّ القصيدة الأصلية وغنتها المطربة المصرية المعروفة فايزة أحمد

لم تعد ذاكراً عهود هوانا
كيف كنا وحبنا كيف كانا

يا حبيبي.. نسيت ايام حبي
ووعوداً تهفو إليك حناناً

بيتنا طائر الدروب غريب
يسأل الليل والضحى عن لقانا

قد بنينا للحب دنيا وفاءٍ
وعلى الحب قد تجنت يدانا

حبنا... حبنا غمامة صيف
وسراب تمضي إليه خطانا

فيه ذقنا مرارة وجفاء
وكفانا من مره ما كفانا

يا حبيبي سألت عنك الليالي
والليالي مُرددات صدانا

عد مع الفجر باسماً للأماني
ليس للحب يا حبيبي سوانا

Laugh

She laughed
and I was surrounded by fragrance
A morning broke, a splendid sight!

Who has taught ivory to be dissipated
taking a path
with the twilight…!

A mouth…
like a handful of lilies
poured all the blisses and darted away

like a flower vase…
a pool… a glass
that quivered and was spilled

she laughed
and sprinkled my room
with roses… jasmine… basil

Her mouth was a blossoming call…
her mouth…
Oh, the lovely leaves

A dawn
once called on me
Its voice went hoarse, and it was choked

Do not ask me…
about its name!
about its color…!
or how it emerged…!

It is a reckless mouth
Oh Lord…!
What a creation…!

ضحكة

ضحكتْ..
فطوّقني العَبَقْ
وانشقّ صبحٌ وأتلقْ

من علّم العاجَ الأباحةَ
فاستحمّ
مع الشّفقْ..!

ثغرٌ..
كحفنة زنبقٍ
دّفق المباهجِ وانطلقْ

كإناءِ ورِدٍ..
بركةٌ..
كأسٌ تهزهز، واندلقْ

ضحكتْ..
ورشّتْ حجرتي
ورداً.. وفلاًّ.. وحبقْ

فمها نداءٌ مزهرٌ..
فمها...
وما أحلى الورقْ

فجرٌ...
دعاني مرّةً..
فانبحّ همسه، واختنقْ

لا تسألوني..
ما اسْمُهُ؟
ما لونه..؟
كيف انبققْ..!؟

هذا فمٌ مستهترٌ
ويلاه ربي..!
ما خلقْ..!

Anwar Salman

Selections From

Colored Cards For An Age With No Festive Days
(1995)

مختارات من ديوان

بطاقات ملوّنة
لزمن بلا أعياد

(1995)

A Bouquet Of Flowers For Her Birthday

She said:
My friend, I've known you as a poet
and poems are the roses of festive days
If I asked for a bouquet of words
what would you give me? Tomorrow is my birthday!

And I replied
as her words in my ears rang
just like a message arriving unforeseen:
Those festive days with us toy… pilfer our days,
and we love them as innocent boys…!
But have you come
when my limbs are so weary
when embers have been put out by piles of ash...?
On my lips words of love no more to pass
nor rosy poems will be for them to chant
Laden with longing,
my notebooks I have closed, and held them as a moon for
my homeland's wound

باقةَ وَرد لِعيد ميلاده

قالَتْ:
عَرَفْتُكَ يا صَديقي شاعِراً،
والشِّعْرُ وَرْدُ مَحَافِلِ الأعْيادِ.
لَوْ جِئْتُ أطْلُبُ مِنْ كَلامِكَ باقَةً،
ماذا سَتُهْدِيني؟... غداً ميلادي!

فَأَجَبْتُها،
وَحَدِيثُها في مَسْمَعي
كَرِسالَةٍ وَصَلَتْ بِلا مِيعَاد:
تَلهو بِنا الأعْيادُ.. تَسْرِقُ عُمْرَنَا،
وَنُحِبُّها بِبَراءَةِ الأوْلادِ!...
هَلْ جِئْتِني،
وَجَوارِحي مُنْهَدَّةٌ،
والجَمْرُ أطفَأَةُ رُكَامُ رَمَادِي؟
لَمْ يَبْقَ في شِفَتي كَلامٌ لِلهَوى
وَقَصائِدٌ وَرْدِيَّةُ الإنْشَادِ.
فَأنا..
طَوَيْتُ عَلى الحَنينِ دَفاتِري،
وَحَمَلْتُها قَمَراً لِجُرحِ بلادي

Interval

I love this land… and for it I have sung
my sweetest chants, but does it remember?

For its sun I open my chest… for I have
a morrow that blossoms not without light.

I am my homeland… its visage… its voice
and all that ages have stored therein.

The color of my wounds is its summer,
and all the rest is its rainy season.

فاصلة

عشقْتُ هذي الأرض... غنّيْتُها
أحلى أناشيدي، فهلْ تذكُرُ.

لشمسها أُشْرِعُ صدري... فَلِيْ
غدٌ بغيرِ الضّوءِ لا يُزْهِرُ.

أنا بلادي... وجهُها... صوتُها،
وما بها تختزنُ الأعصُرُ.

لونُ جراحي فصلُ صيفٍ لها،
وما تبقَّى... فصلُها المُمْطِرُ.

Said The Storyteller

I have a country
about whom we've been told
the sweetest tales.
A wall of mountains she is…
that the wind has crowned with clouds,
Spikes have perched on her hands.
It's a land… described by the blue books
in which God
sent his word
to the people
as a piece carved from the magic of paradise…
to whom belong
the swing of the sun and the tomes of clouds.
The hand of the sea… in ancient times
released her as an olive branch in the peak of a dove.
~ ~ ~ ~
But when the storyteller
concludes his tales
and we go to bed,
we glimpse a tear in the eye of the messages!
and see the hands that raise the flags of peace
open fire on
all the words!

قال الرّاوي

لي بلادٌ،
جاء عنها، في الحكاياتِ التي تُروى لنا،
أحلى الكلامْ.
فهي أسوارُ جبالٍ... توَّجَتْها الرّيحُ بالغَيْمِ
وحطَّتْ فوق كفَّيْها السّنابلْ،
وهي أرضٌ... صوَّرَتْها الكُتُبُ الزُّرقُ التي حملها الله
إلى الناسِ
الرّسائل
قطعةٌ من سِحْرِ فردوسٍ... لها
أرجوحةُ الشمس، وأسفارُ الغَمامْ.
ويدُ البحرِ... قديماً،
أطلَقَتْها غُصْنَ زيتونٍ بمنقارِ الحمامْ.

~ ~ ~

غيرَ أنا،
عندما يُنهي لنا الرّاوي الحكاياتِ
ونمضي لننامْ،
نلمحُ الدَّمعةَ في عين الرّسائل!
ونرى الأيدي التي ترفعُ راياتِ السلامْ
تُطلِقُ النارَ على
كلِّ الكلامْ!

On The Margin Of Dialogue

My friend
Since we were born
in this country we have been
mere sheep on sale
in a Thursday
or a Sunday market
which they have made the blessing of festivities in all people's eyes
they've distributed them… they've classified them
by number.
They've fattened them … and so their prices have escalated.

~ ~ ~ ~

And thus, my friend,
this country has been manipulated:
the sheep in this flock is to flourish
the sheep in that flock is to diminish
as the "formula" dictates.
We have no choice!
So why
waste time going on
in the labyrinths of dialogue.

على هامش الحوار

يَا صَديقي.
مُنْذُ كُنَّا،
نَحْنُ في هَذا البَلَدْ
غَنَمٌ مَعْرُوضَةٌ لِلْبَيْعِ في سُوقِ
خَميسٍ،
أوْ أحَدْ!
جَعَلُوهَا نِعْمَةَ الأعْيَادِ في عَيْنِ الجَميعْ.
وَزَّعُوهَا ... صَنَّفُوهَا
بالعَدَدْ.
سَمَّنُوهَا ... فَغَلا سِعْرُ المَبيعْ .

~ ~ ~ ~

هَكذا - يا صَاحِبي-
هُمْ رَتَّبُوا هَذا البَلَدْ:
تَنْقُصُ الأغْنَامُ في هَذا القَطيعْ.
تَكْثُرُ الأغْنَامُ في ذَاكَ القَطيعْ.
مِثْلَمَا «الصِّيغَةُ» تَقْضي.
مَا لَنَا أيُّ خَيارْ!
فَلِمَاذا
نَقْتُلُ الوَقْتَ، وَنَمْضي
في مَتَاهاتِ الحِوارْ

Wounds

The sun of wounds will never set
for from the wound the impossible is born.

He who claims a throne cares not
whether his path is long or short!

My homeland, you've always been a soil
kneaded with blood from our veins.

A nation that's never embraced a wound
is a heavy burden on the land.

جراح

ما لشمسِ الجراحِ، يوماً، أُفُولُ.
فَمِنَ الجُرْحِ يولَدُ المستحيلُ.

لا يُبالي مَنْ راح يطلُبُ مُلْكاً،
يقصُرُ الدَّرْبُ دونَه أم يطولُ!

وطني... أنتَ، منذُ كنتَ، ترابٌ
بدمٍ مِنْ عروقنا مجبولُ.

كلُّ شعبٍ ما عانقَ الجرحَ يوماً،
هو عبءٌ على الترابِ ثقيلُ.

The Train

When the rulers on earth disagree
about
the shape
of the homeland

and war among the people of the world becomes
a tool
for dialogue

and the clouds of time do not pour sun water
in the well of time

Here
the tragedy in history takes
the shape
of a train

from which the smoke of night ascends
in the plains
of the day

القطار

عندما يختلف القادة في الارض
على
شكل
الوطن

وتصير الحرب بين الناس في الدنيا
اداة
للحوار

وغمام الوقت لا يسكب ماء الشمس
في بئر الزمن

عند هذا
تاخذ المأساة في التاريخ
شكلا
لقطار

صاعد منه دخان الليل في
سهل
النهار

The Christ Of The Nation

Crucified upon the prayers of a bleeding wound
drinking the drops of burning tears
Oh how you've been murdered a thousand times
my homeland
but did not take revenge!

How you've accepted to be the history
of red blood on our yellow pages
and never wearied

How in your defeat
You've borne the cross of oppression for the whole nation
And never wearied!

مسيح الشعب

على صلوات جرح نازح تصلب
ومن قطرات دمع محرق تشرب
فكيف قتلت الاف من المرات
يا وطني
ولم تثأر

وكيف قبلت ان تبقى على اوراقنا
الصفراء تاريخ الدم الاحمر

ولم تتعب

وكيف حملت مهزوما
صليب القهر عن شعب بكامله
ولم تتعب

A Question

You pass as a broken sword on my eyelids,
though yesterday you were a hand that picked the moon…!

In the shade of your wound… grief became our date,
until on our eyelashes it turned into trees.

I asked the night in your eyes, O my homeland:
Who is it who loves to travel upon your wounds?

Your silence responded… that in my dialogue
I'm like one who tries to make a stone talk…!

سؤال

تمرُّ سيفاً على جفنيَّ منكسراً،
وكنتَ بالأمس كفّاً تقطُفُ القمرا...!

في ظلِّ جُرْحكِ... صار الحزنُ موعدنا،
حتَّى استحالَ على أهدابنا شجرا.

سألتُهُ... اللّيل في عينيكَ يا وطني:
على جراحكَ... من ذا يعشَقُ السَّفرا؟

فردَّ صمتُكَ... أني في محاورتي
كمنْ يحاولُ أن يستنطقَ الحجرا...!

A Face For Another Homeland

So long as you're for me a journey with dreams...
an illusion
a little imagination
and words!

So long as your face is a biography embossed
with what dealers and rulers ordain…
so long as your border is lost in the distance
and our path
is fraught with thorns and mines…!
So long as you begin and end with glasses
and sleep and wake up in the night of fantasy.
Here is a tear
for your morning from a poet.
Peace be upon you, my homeland.

وجه لوطن آخر

ما دُمتَ لي سفراً مع الأحلامْ...
وهْماً،
وبعضَ تخيُّلٍ،
وكلامْ!
ما دامَ وجهُكَ سيرةً مطبوعةً
بمواقفِ التجّارِ والحُكَّامْ...
ما دامَ حدُّكَ في المسافَةِ ضائعاً.
وطريقُنا
مزروعةً بالشَّوْكِ والألغامْ...!
ما دُمتَ تبدأُ في الكؤوسِ وتنتهي،
وتُفيقُ في ليلِ الهوى وتنامْ.
فإلى صباحِكِ
دمعةٌ من شاعرٍ،
وعليكَ – يا وطَني – التَّحيَّةُ والسّلامْ.

Fog

The earth has turned me round and round
e'er since the beginning of time.

Companion mine the sun has been.

And yet despite my inkwells' singing
and all my steps
upon
my notebooks,

I've never reached the truth.

ضباب

الأرضُ بي تدور
من أول العصورْ.

والشمس لي رفيقةٌ.

وبرغم حدو محابري،
وخطايَ
فوقَ
دفاتري،

لم ابلغ الحقيقةُ.

The Blue Expanse [2]

My eyelids have opened upon a dream
Oh, look around! All this expanse so blue

Extending from east... to west
where I have sails and a canoe.

My visions lead me away as if I were
traveling to the gate of the absolute, so it seems!

If I return... I'll have a horizon in my hands
And if I meet my end… I'll drown in dreams.

المدى الأزرق

مُتَفَتِّحٌ جَفْنِي عَلَى حُلُم.
فَتَلَفُّتِي، هَذا المَدَى الأزرقْ .

مِنْ مَشْرِقِ الدُّنْيَا ... لِمَغْرِبِهَا،
لِي فِيهِ أَشْرِعَةٌ وَلِي زَوْرَقْ.

لَكَأَنَّنِي، وَرُؤَايَ تَبْعُدُ بِي،
سَفَرٌ إلى بَوَّابَةِ المُطْلَقْ!

فَإِذا رَجَعْتُ... فَفِي يَدِي أُفُقٌ،
وَإذا انْتَهَيْتُ... فَفِي الرُّؤَى أَغْرَقْ.

These

In my country there are pretenders,
bands whose thoughts are not accepted on earth
nor in heaven.
They carried pencils for a cause:
They rejected creativity in all literary
ages.
These…
with the alphabets have built towers,
mansions in the air!
When talking to us… they tell us
that what is called legacy
has all turned into smoke, ashes, and rubble.
When trying to surprise us with a novelty,
their paper and their ideas they arrange
with utmost care,
and carry themselves like great writers.
They enter the café in the morning…
and go out in the evening
leaving *talk* inside the café.

هؤلاء

في بلادي أدعياءُ.
زُمَرٌ. لا فكرُهُمْ في الأرض مقبولٌ
ولا عند السّماءِ.
حمَلوا الأقلام من أجلِ قضية.
رفضوا الإبداعَ في كلِّ العصورِ
الأدبيَّةْ.
هؤلاءِ...
عمَّروا بالحَرْفِ أبراجاً،
قصوراً في الهواءِ!
فإذا ما حدَّثونا... أخبرونا
أنَّ ما يُدعى تراثاً،
كلُّه صارَ دخاناً ورماداً ورُكامْ.
وإذا ما حاولوا أن يُتحِفونا بجديدٍ،
رتَّبوا الأوراقَ والأفكار،
في كلِّ اهتمامْ،
ومشوا مثلَ كبارِ الأدباءِ.
دخلوا المقهى صباحاً...
خرجوا عند المساءِ...
تركوا في داخل المقهى الكلامْ

Something Out Of Nothing

From the start of the day till the end
I leave my door wide open
for silence
and ennui.
I sit at my desk,
and practice
depression.
I take a look at my diary… I read about the days.
Nothing in the morning paper to read
The news brought in by the days
are all the same!

~ ~ ~ ~

And lest I fall asleep
and lest my day be stolen by this ennui,
I try to break… my silence
by writing.
My lip:
no roses dwell in its blood
no visions
where oases glow amidst the gloom of thoughts!
I have no choice but to break the pencils.
And thus the dialogue
comes to an end.
and I myself come to an end…
leaving the paper alienated.
For the start of talk is like its end,
and the end of the day is like its start!

شيء من لا شيء

مِنْ أَوَّلِ النَّهَارِ حتَّى آخِرِ النَّهَارْ.
أَتْرُكُ بَابِي مُشْرَعَاً
للصَّمْتِ
وَالرَّتَابَهْ.
أَجْلِسُ خَلْفَ مَكْتَبِي،
أُمَارِسُ
الكَآبَهْ.
أنْظُرُ في يَوْمِيَّتي ... أُطالِعُ الأَيَّامْ.
لا شيْءَ في جَريدَةِ الصَّباح كَيْ أقْرَأَهُ
صَارَ سَوَاءً
كُلُّ ما تَحْمِلُهُ الأَيَّامْ... مِنْ أخْبَارْ!

~ ~ ~ ~

وَخَوْفَ أَنْ أنَامْ.
وَخَوْفَ أن تَسْرِقَ يَوْمِي هَذِهِ الرَّتَابَهْ،
أُحَاوِلُ الخُرُوجَ ... مِنْ صَمْتي
إلى الكِتَابَهْ.
وَشَفَتي
لا وَرْدَ في دِمَائِها،
وَلا رُؤىً
وَاحَاتُها مُضِيئَةٌ في عَتْمَةِ الأَفْكَارْ!
فَلا يَكونُ غيرُ أَنْ أحَطِّمَ الأقْلامْ.
فَيَنْتَهي
الحِوَارْ.
وَأَنْتَهيْ...
لأَتْرُكَ الأَوْرَاقَ في غُرْبَتِهَا
وَأوَّلُ الكَلامِ مثلُ آخِرِ الكَلامْ،
وَآخِرُ النَّهارِ مِثلُ أَوَّلِ النَّهَارْ!

I Don't Want An Apology

This poem won the prize of "The Most Beautiful Song." It was also chosen as the best poem at Carthage Festival, Tunisia, 1994

Be as you wish... oppressive or forgiving
a captive in your hands I will no longer be

The bird that has been locked up for so long
is able now to fly and set itself free

Accuse me of whatever you wish... for I
won't be enraged no matter what you do

The love story, O actor, turned out to be
a great illusion when up the curtain drew

No longer are you a sun in my eyes' sky
nor a roar in the nectar inside my glass

You have been once a beloved friend
the most favored among all my companions

So clear were my position and feelings
but your position and feelings were volatile

Be as you wish... I don't want an apology
O prince
who once
was my prince

Don't tell me you've carpeted my path with roses,
for on their thorns I'm so tired of walking.

In my love for you so often I've seen death
Burn just as often now that I shun you!

Don't send me threats
if you are the first love
in my life... you will not be the last.

لا أريدُ اعتذاراً

القصيدة الفائزة بجائزة أجمل أغنية عربيّة، وأفضل نصّ شعري. في مهرجان قرطاج 1994.

كُنْ كَما شِئْتَ... ظالِماً أوْ غَفُورا.
لَمْ أَعُدْ في يَدَيْكَ قَلْباً أسيرا.

ذَلِكَ الطَّائِرُ السَّجِينُ زَماناً،
أَصْبَحَ الآنَ قادِراً أَنْ يَطِيرا.

إتَّهِمْني بِمَا تَشَاءُ ... فَإنِّي،
مَا تَمَادَيْتَ سَيِّدي، لَنْ أَثُورا.
قِصَّةُ الحُبِّ - يا مُمَثِّلُ - أَمْسَتْ
عِنْدَ رَفْعِ السِّتَارِ... وَهْماً كَبِيرا
لَمْ تَعُدْ في سَماءِ عَيْنَيَّ شَمْساً.
لَمْ تَعُدْ في رَحيقِ كَأْسِي هَديرا.
كُنْتَ لي، مَرَّةً، صَديقاً حَبيباً
وَرَفيقاً بَيْنَ الرِّفاقِ أَثيرا
واضِحاً كانَ مَوْقِفي، وشُعُوري،
وَتَغَيَّرْتَ... مَوْقِفاً وشُعُورا
كُنْ كَما شِئْتَ ... لا أُريدُ اعْتِذاراً
يا أَميراً...
عَلَيَّ
كانَ أَميرا
لا تَقُلْ لي ... فَرَشْتَ دَرْبي وُرُوداً،
فَعَلى شَوكِها مَلَلْتُ المَسيرا.
إنَّني مِتُّ في هَواكَ كَثيراً،
فَاخْتَرِقْ أَنْتَ في صُدُودي كَثيرا
لا تُهَدِّدْ
إنْ كُنْتَ أَوَّلَ حُبٍّ
في حَياتي ... فَلَنْ تَكُونَ الأَخيرا

The Beauty Of Beauties

This poem was set to music and sung by Lebanese singer Mohamed El Etr. It received the first prize at Cairo International Festival for Arabic Songs

Beauty of beauties, in your face
I'm searching for a glorious sun
hidden away by the scarf of clouds

I'm searching for a lost summer star...
that has escaped from the home of stars

In your face there is a charm...
There is temptation
inscribed on all your features

and love poems more beautiful than
the dreams of forest sparrows

Something about your face is different
from the faces of beautiful ladies

and I am a beauty lover ... reciting
prayers in the temple of your eyes!

Your love has changed me... turned me
into a child within a few hours
A child who dreams, who loves, who toys
painting wine-colored lips

who travels as a sailor... who anchors
in a sea of oil-green eyes

My life before you has been a song
looking for a tune, looking for words

before you I didn't fall in love
But I lost so many years

أحلى الحُلوات

لحّنت هذه القصيدة وغنّاها المطرب اللبناني محمد العتر، وقد فازت بالجائزة الأولى في مهرجان القاهرة الدولي للأغنية العربية.

في وَجْهِكِ، يا أَحْلَى الحُلوَاتْ.
أَبْحَثُ عَنْ شَمْسٍ رائِعَةٍ
خَبَّأَهَا مِنْدِيلُ الغَيْمَاتْ.

عَنْ نَجْمَةِ صَيْفٍ ضَائِعَةٍ...
هارِبَةٍ مِنْ بَيْتِ النَّجْمَاتْ!

في وَجْهِكِ سِحْرٌ...
إِغْرَاءٌ
مَكْتُوبٌ في كُلِّ القَسَمَاتْ
وَقَصائِدُ حُبٍّ أَجْمَلُ مِنْ
أَحْلَامِ عَصَافِيرِ الغَابَاتْ

شَيْءٌ في وَجْهِكِ ... مُخْتَلِفٌ
عَنْ كُلِّ وُجُوهِ الحَسْنَاوَاتْ

وَأَنا عَاشِقُ حُسْنٍ ... يَتْلُو
في مَعْبَدِ عَيْنَيْكِ الصَّلَوَاتْ!

غَيَّرَنِي حُبُّكِ ... غَيَّرَنِي.
أَرْجَعَنِي طِفْلاً في سَاعَاتْ.
طِفْلاً يَحْلُمُ، يَعْشَقُ، يَلْهُو
في رَسْمِ شِفَاهٍ خَمْرِيَّاتْ

ويُسَافِرُ بَحَّاراً... يَرْسُو
في بَحْرِ عُيُونٍ زَيْتِيَّاتْ.

أَنا قَبْلَكِ، عُمْرِي أُغْنِيَةٌ
تَبْحَثُ عَنْ نَغَمٍ، عَنْ كَلِمَاتْ.

أَنا قَبْلَكِ لَمْ أَعْشَقْ يَوْمَاً،
لَكِنِّي ... ضَيَّعْتُ السَّنَوَاتْ!

Sailing

Whatever ordeals I pass through
your eyes my homeland will always be

My sun of alphabets towards you will navigate
and illuminate the horizon gate for me.

And in your winds my sails will flap,
your love will be my harbor of melancholy

What matters where the world starts or end…
so long as my vessels sail upon your sea?

The Blue Expanse

إبـحـار

مَهْمَا يَمُرُّ عَلَيَّ مِنْ مِحَنٍ،
عَيْنَاكِ باقِيَتَانِ لِي وَطَني.

شَمْسُ الحُرُوفِ إلَيْكِ تُبْحِرُ بِي،
وَتُضِيءُ لِي بَوَّابَةَ الزَّمَنِ.

وَعَلَى رِيَاحِكِ خَفْقُ أَشْرِعَتِي،
وَيَظَلُّ حُبُّكِ مَرْفَأَ الشَّجَنِ.

مَا أَوَّلُ الدُّنْيَا وآخِرُهَا ...
مَا دَامَ بَحْرُكِ حَامِلاً سُفُنِي!

Anwar Salman

Selections From

I Search In Your Eyes For A Homeland

(2004)

مختارات من ديوان

أبحث في عينيك عن وطن

(2004)

Little Details

I'm all alone
An inkwell lying on my table
like a question!
A little rose
that you gave me
and a chilly night.
A quill whose alphabets offer no warmth
or visions to be told.
A closed notebook
in which a poem
came to a halt at the first line!
And then you come in
like a star
from the window of imagination
and in my alphabets you leave
for love
the most beautiful thing that beauty can ever say!

تفاصيل صغيرة

وحدي.
على طاولتي مِحْبرةٌ
كأنَّها السُّؤال!
ووردةٌ صغيرةٌ منكِ
معي
وليلةٌ باردةٌ.
وريشةٌ لا دِفْءَ في حروفها،
ولا رُؤىً تُقالْ.
ودفترٌ
يُطوَى على قصيدةٍ
توقَّفَتْ في المطلَعِ!
وتدخُلين نجمةً
عليَّ،
من نافذةِ الخيال.
وتتركين في حروفي
للهوى،
أجمل ما يقوله الجمال !

The Runaway Date

What would our meeting bring back to you?
Our tales have drifted away with the past

Gone are they …
We have no yesterday to drop by
that our nostalgic whispers may collect!

No trace of love is there within our hearts
Must we keep looking for what we left behind?

What does it mean to be together,
as though we were counting our sins?

And what use is
our tête-à-tête,
reproach, and the wounds of our complaints?

While you and I were sunk,
in the night of estrangement
our features were forgotten by our mirrors…!

The sky of love went cloudy,
those stars
faded away; our faces were both lost.

The roses of our dreams… dried
they all were scattered,
leaves, boughs and all.

Let's fold away reproach
for
what was yesterday…
has now utterly changed!

الموعد الهارب

ماذا تعيد اليكِ لقيانا؟
ذهبتْ مع الماضيَ حكايانا.

ذهبت...
فما امس نمر به،
وتلمُّه بالشرقِ نجوانا!

لم يبقى منا للهوى أثرٌ،
انظلُّ نبحثُ عن بقايانا؟

ماذا يُفسِّرُ أن نكونَ معًا
وكأننا نُحصي خطايانا!
وحديثُنا
ماذا سينفَعُنا،
وعِتابُنا وجراحُ شكوانا؟

وأنا وأنتِ
بليلِ غُربتنا
نسِيتْ ملامِحَنا مرايانا

غامتْ سماءُ الحبِّ
وانطفأت
تلك النجومُ وضاع وَجْهانا

ووُرودُ أحلامٍ لنا... يبِسَتْ
وتناثرتْ
وَرَقًا وأغصانا.

فلْنطوِ أوراقَ العتابِ
فما
بالأمْسِ كان...
تغيَّرَ الآنا.

The Last Leaf

The last leaf has fallen
off us…
False excuses
are of no use.
~ ~ ~ ~
We tried to get hold of
what's not ours,
but we were defeated…
and lost the bargain.

We planted the dream…
in the balconies of the sun
but we lost all its paths.

We sought all turquoise
from the sea…
but we found it was sunk.

We tore down the garden wall,
 only to pluck a leaf of basil!
~ ~ ~ ~
And now… we return without a shadow
like mercenary thieves of the dawn.

As if we were… in the quiet of the night
two faces in a quivering mirror!

We get drowned in silence
and are exposed
by the looks we steal.

Nothing has been left…
of our story
save burnt paper.

آخر ورقة

سقطت عنا آخر ورقة
سقطت
ما عادت مجدية
كل الأعذار المختلقة.
~ ~ ~ ~
حاولنا ملكاً
ليس لنا
فهزمنا
وخسرنا الصفقة

وزرعنا في شرفات الشمس
الحلم
فضيعنا طرقه

وطلبنا كل الفيروز من
البحر
فواجهنا غرقه
وهدمنا السور على البستان
لكي نقطف منه حبقة
~ ~ ~ ~
والآن نعود بلا ظل
كلصوص الفجر المرتزقة

لكأنا والليل سكون
وجهان بمرآة قلقة

نغرق في الصمت
وتفضحنا
نظرات نسرقها سرقة

لم يبق لنا
من قصتنا
إلا أوراق محترقة

Candles That Give No Light

Like any traveler
I encamp in the evening
on a land
that I imagine to be the homeland of poesy...
when words fail me!
Then I set my tents
thinking that
there
I've gathered my runaway visions
borrowed the doves' cooing for my voice
that I
have settled on the throne of poesy!
~ ~ ~ ~
I light the candles of alphabets around me
and go on
with a thousand colors in my feather,
travelling as a dream with the waves of the inkwell...
disturbing the sleep of all notebooks
and getting drowned –
drowned in the blueness of the dream, that
if I invoke an angel for inspiration
to capture those visions and feelings,
I come back
with fog in the night of my paths
and a mirage and clouds
above my eyelids!
I put out all the candles of words
and stay...
with cigarette ashes
to drop the shadows of curtains around me,
falling asleep upon a line of poetry, on which I reflect

شموع لا تضيء

كأيّ مسافرْ.
أحطُّ الرّحال مساءً،
بأرضٍ
يخيَّل لي أنها وطنُ الشّعر...
حين يصير عصيّاً عليَّ الكلام!
فأضربُ فيها خيامي،
وأحسبُ أني
- عليها -
ضَمَمْتُ الرّؤى الهاربات...
استعَرْتُ لصوتي هديل الحمامْ.
وأنّي
استوَيْتُ على عرشٍ شاعرْ!
~ ~ ~ ~
فأشعلُ حولي شموع الحروف،
وأمضى
وفي ريشتي ألف لونٍ ولونٍ،
أسافر حلْماً بموج الدّواة...
أقضُّ مضاجع كلّ الدفاتر.
وأغرق،
أغرقُ في زُرقَة الحلم، حتى
إذا رحتُ أدعو ملاكاً لِوَحْي
يصوِّر تلك الرؤى والمشاعر،
أعودُ،
وليلُ دروبي ضباب،
وفوق جفوني سرابٌ،
غمامْ!
فأطفئ كلّ شموع الكلامْ.
وأبقى...
أنا ورماد السّجائر،
لأسدلَ حولي ظلال السّتائر،
وفي بيتِ شعرٍ أفكّر فيه أنام.

Sunset

Five stars,
a necklace, a moon,
a canopy of swings of thoughts,

and an evening of love in whose horizon
a sweet girl runs and a long-awaited promise gleams

~ ~ ~ ~

Whenever I open an eyelid in the expanse
memories and pictures
come to mind

I am a night
from whence visions set out,
and love inscribes the history of travel.

I go sailing, asking infinity and
about you,
but… no news!

غروب

خمس نجمات،
وعقد وقمر.
وسرير من أراجيح الفكر.

ومساء عاشق... في افقه
حلوة تعدو، ووعد منتظر.
~ ~ ~ ~
كلما أشرعت جفنا في المدى،
راودتني
ذكريات وصور.

أنا ليل
تبتدي منه الرؤى،
وهوى يكتب تاريخ السفر.

مبحر... أسأل عنك المنتهى،
والمواعيد،
ولكن... لا خبر!

Your Eyes Are Summer Nights

This poem was set to music and sung by Lebanese soprano Majida El Roumi.

Your eyes are summer nights,
visions,
rosy poems!
and love letters running away
from forgotten tomes of passion.
~ ~ ~ ~
Who are you…?
With your nimble steps you've planted
damask roses along the road
As light you've passed…
as pulses of perfume,
as the chanting of popular songs
You've moved like a sail… bearing me
as a poem of a marine sun
towards promises painted by
the dreams of an Oriental young female!
~ ~ ~ ~
Who are you?
The magic in your eyes
fulfills a wish in my life
As though you have come from a moon
or from a golden morning star!
From a land where the sun of love
embraces the face of liberty.

And I am
a traveler in this life
and with me…
are your eyes and a song!

عيناكَ ليالٍ صيفيَّة

هذه القصيدة غنتها المطربة اللبنانية ماجدة الرومي.

عيناكَ ليالٍ صيفيَّهْ،
ورؤىً،
وقصائدُ ورديَّهْ؟
ورسائلُ حبٍّ هاربةٌ
من كُتُبِ الشَّوقِ المنسيَّة.
~ ~ ~ ~

مَنْ أنتَ؟...
زرعْتَ بنقْلِ خُطاكَ
الدَّرْبَ وُروداً جوريَّهْ!
كالضَّوْءِ مررْتَ...
كَخَفْقِ العِطْرِ،
كَهَزْجِ أغانٍ شعبيَّهْ.
ومضيتَ شراعاً... يحمِلُني
كَقصيدةِ شمسٍ بحريَّهْ.
لوعودٍ راحتْ ترسُمُها
أحلامُ فتاةٍ شرقيَّهْ!
~ ~ ~ ~

من أنتَ؟
وسحرٌ في عينيكَ
يزفُّ العمرَ لأُمْنِيَّهْ.
لكأنَّكَ... من قمرٍ تأتي.
من نجمةِ صُبحٍ ذهبيَّهْ!

من أرضٍ... فيها شمسُ الحبِّ
تُعانِقُ وجْهَ الحُريَّهْ.

وأنا...
في العُمرِ مسافرةٌ،
ومعي...
عيناكَ وأغنيَّهْ!

Dreams On The Rhone

On the banks of the Rhone we were in the evening,
and like
every evening
Lac Léman was
a pretty love mirror
for that blue sky.
Geneva was like a stately thicket:
Flower gardens emerging before our eyes
and water sirens coming towards us!
~ ~ ~ ~
On the bank of dreams we were
surrounded by the expanse
with its poetic evening.
The coy Geneva sun
went…
behind a cloud in the horizon
that glowed in red and waned
turning the night of the lake
into a party of perfumes…
banquets of love…
a prayer… a song!
On the surface of the water
Byron's hymns
and Rimbaud's dreams
looked
like wounds!
I saw how…
for poetry to knock on the gate of eternity,
words must bleed!
how poets' quill
lends beauty to this world
then goes away
with nothing
save its wound!

أحلامٌ على الرُّونِ

على ضفَّةِ الرُّونِ كنّا مساءً،
وكانتْ
- كُلَّ مساءٍ -
بُحيرةُ "ليمانَ"
مرآةَ عِشْقٍ جميلهْ
لِزُرْقةِ تلكَ السّماءْ.
وكانت "جنيف" بزَهْوٍ خميلَهْ،
تُطِلُّ علينا حدائقَ وردٍ
وتمشى إلينا عرائسَ ماءْ!
~ ~ ~ ~

على شاطئ الحُلْمِ كنّا،
وكان المدى حوْلنا
شاعريَّ المساءْ.
وشمسُ "جنيف" الخجولةُ
راحَتْ...
وراء غمامةِ أفْقٍ،
تشفُّ احمراراً وتخبو.
لتترُكَ ليلَ البحيرةِ
حفلَ طيوبٍ...
موائدَ عشقٍ...
صلاةً... عناءْ!
وكانتْ...
على صفحةِ الماءِ لي تتراءى
جراحاً،
أناشيدُ "بايْرونْ"
وأحلامُ "رامبو!"
وكنتُ أشاهدُ كيف...
لكيْ يطرُقَ الشِّعرَ بابَ خلودٍ،
من الكلماتِ تسيلُ الدّماءْ!
وكيف تزوِّدُ هذا الوجودَ جمالاً،
وتمضى وليس لديها
سوى جُرْحِها... ريشةُ الشُّعراءْ!

A Sailor

In your eyes
I scattered my alphabets' sun
upon the flaps of a beautiful sail

and searched between them for a homeland!

In your eyes I've been traveling…
for a long time to get there

And I'm still sailing upon the passage of time!

بَحّار

بعينيك ،
رحت أبعثر شمس حروفي
على خفقات شراع جميل.

وأبحث لي فيهما عن وطن!

بعينيك كنت المسافر...
كم طال بي زمن للوصول،

وما زلت أبحر فوق مرور الزمن!

A More Beautiful Morrow

Out of the moon of sorrows
out of fire and smoke
I've gathered you from a red wound
and painted you in green
above the whiteness of snow
And there they were
your face… your voice…
your heart
O Lebanon!

غدٌ أجمل

مِنْ قَمَرِ الأحزانْ.
مِنْ نارٍ ودخانْ.
لَمْلَمْتُكَ من جُرحٍ أحمرْ.
ورسمْتُكَ باللّونِ الأخضرْ،
فوقَ بياضِ الثَلجِ،
فكانْ
وجهكَ... صوتُك...
قلبُكَ،
يا لبنان!

Anwar Salman

A Piece From Heaven

Like you no painting has ever been
nor a mind has visualized

On these peaks
you are
akin to stars that write beauty

In the expanse…
whenever your shady
mountainside smiles

and your plain land folds the flag
from the south
to the north

I say:
I have a glorious homeland
It is these mountains

قطعةٌ من سماء

مثلكَ... الرسم ما رسمْ
لا... ولا صور الخيالْ

أنتَ في هذه القمم
انجمٌ تكتب الجمال

في المدى...
كل ما ابتسمْ
سفحك الوارف الظلالْ

وطوى سهلك العلمْ
من جنوبٍ
الى شمالٍ
قلت:
لي موطن اشمْ
انه هذه الجبال!

Prime Of Life

My homeland is love…
Is there a heart
that has a sweeter date
or a lovelier bosom?

I have a country…
the sun had kissed
before there ever were love or kisses!

For art she is a horizon of visions
Thus she's been since the beginning of time.

Upon her eyelids light was born.
Her land is made of stars and eyes.

Her high peaks,
if they ever fall,
will be received by the bosom of a hero!

عنفوان

وطني الحبُّ...
فهل قلب له
موعد احلى،
وصدر اجمل؟

لي بلاد...
قبلة الشمس لها،
قبل ان كان الهوى والقبل!

فهي للابداع افاق رؤى،
وهي كانت منذ كان الازل.

ولد الضوء على اجفانها.
فثراها انجم او مقل.

وذراها السُمر...
ان يوما هوت،
يتلقاها بصدر بطل!

Giving

Out of the ringing of the hard pickaxe
upon these rocks,

and the dance of a quill
that loves to write with light

Our hands carved
our dream… on every grain of soil

Our generations have proliferated
thought throughout the eons.

My country,
since it existed,

has been holding the sun in its hand
while the earth revolved!

عطاء

من رنين المعول الصلب
على هذي الصخور،

وتثني ريشةٍ
نعشق بالضوء الكتابة.

نقشت أيدٍ لنا
الحلم... على كل ترابة!

نشرت أجيالنا
الفكر... على مر العصور.

وبلادي...
منذ في الأزمان كانت،

تحمل الشمس على كفٍ
وبالأرض تدور!

The Anthem Of Roses And The Sun

Above fire I write your name
above roses
above laurels

I write it above the sun mirrors
above the foreheads of free men.
~ ~ ~ ~
Rise.
Who said that dreams turn into smoke?!

Rise from the clouds of the wounds' blood,
and from the silence of sorrows.

Come back, a sweet green homeland…
never to be defeated… or vanquished!

Rise
unite, and gain your freedom.
Make your own history…
my homeland
out of the nation's unity and determination.
~ ~ ~ ~
You are a treasure of pride
and beauty for your nation.
A king you are… cedars are your crown, heroes are your men!

Ascend your future
the flag and torch are for your hands.

You are always the greatest love
the anthem of roses…
and of the sun
my glory
my laurels on earth!

نشيد الورد والشمس

اكتب اسمك فوق النار.
فوق الورد،
وفوق الغار

اكتبه فوق مرايا الشمس،
وفوق جباه الاحرار.
~ ~ ~ ~

انهض.
من قال يصير الحلم دخان؟!

انهض من غيم دم الجرح،
وصمت الاحزان.

وارجع وطنا حلوا اخضر...
وطنا لا يهزم... لا يقهر!

انهض.
وتوحد وتحرر.
واصنع تاريخك...
يا وطني،
من وحدة شعب وقرار
~ ~ ~ ~

انت لشعبك كنز
من عز وجمال.
ملك تاجك... ارز ورجالك ابطال!

فكن الصاعد للمستقبل
ليديك الراية والمشعل.

ابدا... انت الحب الاجمل
ونشيد الورد...
ونشيد الشمس،
ومجدي
في الارض وغاري

A Procession

The peaks sailing in the blue horizon
a mast embracing the unknown…

 Akin to them is our people breaking into the depth of the wound
and moving… directly on its path.

Born from the torch of eternity we are
We've grown up not knowing the impossible.

We are the masters of self-sacrifice,
each generation training the next generation.

مسيرة

الذرى المبحرات في زرقة الأفق
شراعا يعانق المجهولا

مثلها شعبنا يشق مدى الجرح
ويمضي توجها وسببيلا

نحن من شعلة البقاء ولدنا
فنشأنا لا نعرف المستحيلا
واحترفنا الفداء حتى غدونا
كل جيل منا يعلم جيلا

A Cloudy Sky

My homeland, in the sky of my thoughts you are
a dream tied to the wings of a bird!

The sun's longing grows leaves in the soil
and your visage remains as raining clouds.

My homeland, you turn your face towards the morn
but in the raging conflict lost you are

You've lived in all bullets… as if
in the bag of a rebel you've hidden your sun!

سماء غائمة

وطني كأنك في سماء خواطري
حلم تعلق في جناحي طائر!

الشمس يورق في التراب حنينها
ويظل وجهك كالغمام الماطر

وطني وأنت إلى الصباح تلقّتُ
وتضيع في ليل الصراع الدائر.

كل الرصاص سكنته... لكأنما
خبأت شمسكَ في حقيبة ثائر !

Anwar Salman

Selections From

The Poem Is An Impossible Woman

(2008)

مختارات من ديوان

القصيدة امرأة مستحيلة

(2008)

A Green Quill

You are my star
Keep my night illuminated
when
my days are transformed into travel.
I write with light
My pages are a sky
that has drunk
the seasons
from the color of your eyes
I've always carried the sun with me
while…
painting an impossible dream
I'd never loved night
until
you became the green quill
and lovely poetry

ريشة خضراء

نجمتي أنتِ.
دَعي ليلي مُضاءً،
عندما
تصبحُ أيّامي رحيلاً.
إنني أكتبُ بالضَّوْءِ،
وأوراقي سماءٌ
شربَتْ
مِنْ لونِ عينَيْكِ
الفُصُولا.
كنتُ دوماً
أحملُ الشَّمْسَ معي،
وأنا...
أرسُمُ حُلْماً مستحيلاً.
ما عشِقْتُ اللَّيْلَ...
إلاَّ عندما
صِرْتِ أنتِ الرِّيشةَ الخضراءَ،
والشِّعْرَ الجميلا!

A Song For A Passer-By

You walk with pride like a gazelle,
your steps composing a delightful tune.

With you the evening has love dates
and the road is filled with a fragrant scent.

The features of yours face sprouted leaves in my imagination
and were about to write upon my eyelids!
~ ~ ~ ~
You walk wearing your beauty and allure
a silken scarf and golden hair

In your eyes the stars place their pillows to sleep
and flowers on hills celebrate your bosom

Oh you…
Sister of roses, take a look
I am the one who sings for beauty and youth.

Who told you I do not return greetings
that you pass by
without saying hello?!

أغنية الى عابرة

تمشين... تختالين زهوا كالظبا،
ويصوغ وقع خطاك لحنا مطربا.

منك المساء له مواعيد الهوى،
وبك الطريق تفوح عطرا طيبا.

قسمات وجهك في خيالي اورقت،
وعلى جفوني اوشكت ان تكتبا!

~ ~ ~ ~

تمشين... تعتمرين حسنك والغوى
شالا حريرا وشعرا مذهبا.

مدت بعينيك النجوم وسادها،
وبصدرك احتفلت ازاهير الربا.

يا انت...
يا اخت الورود تلفتي.
انا من يغني للجمال وللصبا.

من قال إني لا ارد تحية،
حتى تمري،
لا تقولي مرحبا؟!

A Prayer Outside The Church

On a Sunday morning
as I rambled
along the road near the town church…

she passed as a cloud!
as a hare chased in a forest!

So fast she went… as if
afraid to miss the train.
Or maybe she was late for a date
that she almost revealed
with a touch of melancholy on her face.

But after a while she stopped…
Her eyes
were haunted with dreams and secrets.

No one attracted her attention!

How pretty she was…
When I passed by her
I felt so envious
of that lover
who dated her
for all her beauty.

But as I went on
I fancied her
walking beside me
although she was still standing there
at a waiting station –

that one who
came to pray
on that Sunday!

صلاة خارج الكنيسة

صباح يوم احد،
وكنت أمضى عابرا
فى شارع عند كنيسة البلد...

مرت كما سحابة!
كأرنب مطارد فى غابة!

مسرعة... كأنها
تخاف ان يفوتها القطار.
او انها
تأخرت عن موعد
توشك ان تقوله
فى وجنتيها مسحة الكآبة.

لكنها بعد قليل وقفت...
فى مقلتيها
نظرة مسكونة بالحلم والاسرار.

لم تلتفت الى احد!

فاتنة...
حين مررت قربها،
حسدت فى جمالها
عاشقها
الذي وعد.

وبعدما تابعت سيري،
خلتها
تمشى معى،
ولم تزل واقفة هناك
فى محطة انتظار...

تلك التى
جاءت الى صلاتها
ذاك الاحد!

A Telephone Call

A telephone call
awakened me before it rang,
when all the eyes had gone to sleep

Who could it be?
Warm whispers and longing quivered
in my receiver.

Borne as a song I was by your voice
that came back after all those years.
~ ~ ~ ~
The words enveloped me with fragrance…
in whose gentle breeze my heart flew.
Your voice, coming
on the waves of ether,
extended for me a jasmine swing.

It filled my hearing with a tune
that carried the sweetest lovers' tales.

When will we be together…? sang my date.
Coming back…?
Please say: tomorrow… after tomorrow.
Coming back…? Please say you are,
even if you aren't.

For I have a heart that keeps the promises of love
And the most beautiful …
in the paths of life, are those that have not come!

تلفون

هاتف
أيقظني قبل الرنين،
بعدما اغفت عيون الساهرين.

من ترى؟
وارتعشت في هاتفي
همسات دافئات وحنين.

ومضى يحملني اغنية
صوتك العائد من تلك السنين.

~ ~ ~ ~

كلمات طوقتني بالعبير...
راح في انسمها قلبي يطير.
صوتك الاتي
على موج الاثير
مد لي ارجوحة من ياسمين،

وتهادى ملء سمعي نغما
حاملا احلى حكايا العاشقين

لمتى القاك...؟ غنى موعدي.
راجع...؟
قل لي غدا... بعد غد.
راجع...؟ قلها،
ولو لم تعد.

ان لي قلبا على الحب امين
ومواعيد الهوى... اجملها
في دروب العمر، وعد لا يحين!

Childhood

Little kids we were
when you and I met.
You were prettier than a bashful violet flower,
Together we walked,
and life was a school
for childhood dreams!

~ ~ ~ ~

Years passed by…
After a while we became friends…
Or was it love?
I do not know…
But every time we met,
we tried
to stay longer together.

And there were silent words
between our hearts.
Oh, how we both
wished to say them!

But it was just
a timid wish
and on we went
without dreams,
that it remained impossible.

Oh Lord… That childhood
of love…
How sweet it was!

طفولة

طفلين كنا،
والتقينا
كنت اجمل من بنفسجة خجولة
ومعا ترافقنا،
وكان العمر مدرسة
لاحلام الطفولة

~ ~ ~ ~

وتوالت الاعوام...
صرنا بعد حين اصدقاء...
أو كان حباً؟
لست ادري...
انما في كل ميعاد لنا،
كنا نحاول
ان يطول بنا اللقاء.

وحديث صمت
بين قلبينا
كلانا
كم تمنى ان يقوله.

لكنها امنية
بقيت خجولة.
ومعا مضينا
دون احلام،
وظلت مستحيلة.

الله... كم تلك الطفولة
- في الهوى -
كانت جميلة!

Silent Music

No warmth is there in the memory,
Do not scatter my notebooks
to read the poems
that yesterday
I jotted down.

The seasons of roses have passed by,
my friend,
we cannot carry on
till the end of the road!

~ ~ ~ ~

What use is it to go back to the paper
in our drawers…
when the words in those lines
are cold,
and all that moves our longing
for love…
is playing on a guitar
with broken strings?

معزوفة صامتة

لا دفء في الذكرى
فلا تعبُثري دفاتري
لتقرئي ماذا كتبت فوقها
بالأمس،
من أشعار.

مرت فصول الورد
يا صديقتي،
ولم يعد بوسعنا
أن نكمل المشوار!

~ ~ ~ ~

ما نفع أن نعود للأوراق
في أدراجنا...؟
حين الكلام في السطور
بارد،
وكل ما يحرك الحنين فينا
للهوى...
عزف على قيثارة
مقطوعة الأوتار!

Ink On Paper

You had the most beautiful face
for painting,
but never were you a woman for poetry.
I do recall that,
since I knew you,
I haven't written about you…
even a single line!
Nothing distinguishes a rose…
save the fragrance it holds.

I apologize
if I passed by
and wasn't enchanted
by your magic.
For there are women
written in poetry
and other women
whom ink does drink.

حبر على ورق

كنت الوجه الأجمل
للرسم،
وما كنت امرأة للشعر.

أتذكر أني
منذ عرفتك
لم أكتب عنك...
ولو سطر!

لا يعطي الوردة إيثارا...
إلا ما تحمله من عطر.
عذرا،
إن كنت مررت عليك
ولم يأخذني
هذا السحر

فهناك امرأة
تُكتَب شعرا
وامرأة
يشربها الحبر!

A Play

For Sai'd Takieddine[3]

I was there!
A whole hour passed

I did not understand
what on the stage was going on

Around me there was a lot of noise… a lot of clamor…
idiotic laughs among the crowd

No one in the hall
was listening.

The audience were there
but their ears
were still
outside the theater gates!

~ ~ ~ ~

Everyone was in their seat
and chaos was everywhere.

The stage reveled as it flared
with lights and colors.

In silence I pondered
Oh how those ears
Elongated!

مسرحية
الى سعيد تقي الدين

كنت هناك،
ومرت ساعة.

لم أفهم شيئا
مما فوق المسرح كان يدور!

من حولي صخب... ضوضاء...
ضحكات بلهاء لحضور.

لا أحد في القاعة
يصغي.

كان الجمهور هناك،
وكانت آذان الجمهور
ما زالت
خارج أبواب القاعة!

~ ~ ~ ~

كلٌ في مقعده كان،
الفوضى في كل مكان.

والمسرح يزهو محتفلاً
بالأضواء وبالألوان.

وأنا أتأمل في صمت...
كم طالت
تلك الآذان!

Custody

Messengers told us
and prophets too
that sovereignty and power
on Earth
are in the custody of Man
No one is above him
save the majesty of God in the highest heaven
who owns the mysteries of the universe and of being and
who alone
directs them as he wills…
And since then
Man
has been driven by his whims

exercising his power
with arrogance

Whenever indulging in sins
he ascribes them to heaven.

وصاية

قالت لنا الرسل
وقال الأنبياء
الملك فوق الأرض
والسلطان
في عهدة الإنسان
وفوقه لا أحدٌ
إلا جلال الله في عليائه
مالك أسرار الوجود والبقاء
وحده
يديرها كما يشاء...
ومنذ ذاك الحين
والإنسان
يمضي على أهوائه...

ممارساً سلطانه
في كبرياء

وكلما أسرف في أخطائه
يحيلها على السماء

A Traveler

When your vision
sails
towards
a distant
land

searching for an age
painted
by the dreams
of a poet

Don't go as a guest
into
the house
of the poem

Your port of dreams
is
endless traveling

مسافر

عندما
تبحر في الرؤيا
إلى
دنيا
بعيدة

باحثاً عن زمنٍ
ترسمه
أحلام
شاعر

لا تكن ضيفا
على
بيت
القصيدة

مرفأ الأحلام
أن
تبقى المسافر.

The Bird Of Ink

He passed like a migrating bird…
bearing the sky upon his wings!

Bearing in its eyes a summer,
roses,
stars,
and an evening.

Planting the horizon with dates
and happy dreams,
planting mawwals [4]
on the chords of distant
travels.

Sometimes…
he'd raise his wings above the clouds
Sometimes he'd glide slowly… descending
and landing on a bough
where he enjoys to show off,
chant,
and sing!

That one searching in his travels
for a new sun
for his world
in a space without a beginning or end…

Was a poet

From whose eyelid the dreams fell off
at night
and he never finished the poem

طائر الحبر

مر كالطير المسافر ...
حاملا فوق جناحيه السماء !

حاملا صيفا بعينيه ،
ووردا ،
ونجوما
ومساء .

يزرع الافق مواعيدا
واحلاما سعيدة .
ومواويل
على اوتار اسفار
بعيدة .

مرة ...
يُعلي على غيمٍ جناحيه
وآنا يتهادى ... هابطا
يحتل غصنا
فوقه يحلو له زهو
وشدو ،
وغناء !

ذلك الباحث في الاسفار
عن شمس لدنياه ...
جديدة ،
في فضاء ما له بدء واخر ...

كان شاعر

سقطت عن جفنه الاحلام ،
في ليل ،
ولم ينه القصيدة

Composition

In November
When the leaves
fall off the trees

And the sun bashfully veils
his face…
with the scarves of the clouds

Our days…
in Beirut
are spent in waiting and boredom.

Our nights move on
with cold insomnia
that plants no dreams in the sleepers' eyelids.

They come and go
Like a book that passes through our hands
composed of pages
from which words have run away!

تأليف

عندما
تسقط في تشرين
أوراق الشجر.

وتغطي وجهها الشمس
حياءً...
بمناديل الغمام.

تصبح الأيام...
في بيروت
أوقات انتظار وضجر.

ولياليها بنا تمشي
سهاداً بارداً،
لا يزرع الأحلام في جفن النيام!

إنما تأتي وتمضي،
مثلما يعبر أيدينا كتاب
ألفته صفحات
هارب منها الكلام!

Waiting For A Visa

How beautiful it would be
if the Earth were
for all people
a free homeland with no restrictions!

Where every human has a little earth
from which he's come,
and to which he will
return one day!

So why have they deformed this world?
dividing us
parting humans from each other
binding us with passports

Imposing on us rules,
norms,
and other confines…

Transforming homelands
on Earth
into prisons
connected by the thorns of borders!

بانتظار تأشيرة سفر

كم جميل
لو تكون الأرض
للناس جميعا،
وطنا حرا بلا أي قيود.

كل إنسان له فيها تراب
جاء منه،
وهو في يوم
اليه سيعود!

فلماذا شوهوا هذا الوجود؟...
قسمونا...
باعدوا بين البشر
قيدونا بجوازات السفر.

حكموا فينا قوانين،
وأعرافا،
وأسبابا أخر...

جعلوا من هذه الأوطان
في الأرض
سجونا
واصل ما بينها شوك الحدود!

Anwar Salman

Selections From

Mirrors For Runaway Dreams

(2017)

مختارات من ديوان

**مرايا
لأحلام هاربة**

(2017)

Traveling With The Sail Of The Sun

Take me on your flying wing…

Take me to all the skies, where hundreds of moons plant me in the eyelids of wakefulness, where millions of stars sprinkle me with light in the gardens of dreams…!

Let me, O sun, hear the echo of the earth's prayer to your abundant warmth… so that I may feel – while she embraces me – that what comes from her depths roaring, is the sound of my triumph, rebellion, and faith…!

Teach me, O princess of the throne of heaven,[5] embroidered with the most wonderful eternal poetry, which had been borne upon beds of magical melodies before the fairies of love had their own time and era…! Teach me daily how to weave from the gold of your eyelids a bracelet for a little girl whose agony unites with your traveling seconds, and a ball for a little boy frightened by the cooing of fire in the trees of childhood gardens…!

سفرٌ في شراعِ الشمس

خُذيني على جناحكِ الطائر....

خُذيني إلى كلِّ السّمواتِ، حيثُ آلافُ الأقمارِ تزرعُني في جُفونِ السَّهر، وحيثُ ملايينُ النُّجوم تَرُشُّ عليَّ الضَّوْءَ في حدائقِ الأحلامِ...!

أسمِعيني... يا شَمْسُ.. صَدى صلاةِ الأرض لِدِفْئِكِ الغامِر... علَّني – وأنا في أحضانِها – أشعُرُ أنَّ ما يَهدُرُ آتياً من أعماقِها هو صوتُ انتصاري وتمرُّدي وإيماني....!

علِّميني... يا أميرةَ عرشِ السماءِ المُوشَّى بأروَعِ كلماتِ الشِّعرِ الخالِد، والمَحْمولِ على أسِرَّةِ الأنغامِ السّاحرةِ من قبل أن يكونَ لِجنِّيّاتِ الحبِّ عصرٌ وزمان....!
علِّميني كيف كلَّ يومٍ أغزلُ من ذهَبِ أهدابكِ، إسوارةً لطفلةٍ يتَّحِدُ حزنُها بثوانيكِ المُسافرة، وكُرةً لِصَبيٍّ يُخيفُه هديلُ النّارِ في أشجارِ حدائقِ الطُّفولةِ...!

Thunder And Lightning

One natural scientist said:

When I was a child… I thought it was thunder rather than lightning that killed people. As I grew up, I learned that it was lightning, not thunder, that killed people.

Since then, I have decided to be both thunder and lightning, but without being an assassin!

رعْدٌ وبرْق

قالَ أحدُ علماءِ الطَّبيعة:

لمّا كنتُ حدَثاً... كنتُ أتصوّر أنّ الرَّعدَ هو الذي يقتلُ الناس، وليس البرق. ولمّا كبرت، علِمْتُ أنَّ البرق هو الذي يقتل وليسَ الرعد.

ومنذُ ذلك الحين، قرَّرتُ أن أكون الرَّعدَ والبرق معاً، ولكنْ من غير أن أكون القاتل!

Departure

I ascend the stairs of roses... at the entrance of the abandoned home. I am received by roses thirsty for water, yearning for a hand to touch their petals with kindness and to spread on the soil the light of eyes and night tales!

Beautiful houses like these… in whose gardens the seasons of flowers and fragrance have arisen, were for me homes of friends and beloved ones… before they took the train of departure and migrated.

All the houses abandoned by their residents have tales akin to the tale of this house on whose antique stairs I lose my steps, and from whose high evening places memories set sail.

Ah… stairs of nostalgia climbing up the distances to reach the estrangement of those who planted on its sides the travails of their life, and departed without a passport.

Ah, how your waiting resembles grief in those eyes that extend their eyelashes as bridges for return… whenever the night of distance turns its eyelids into a lake of tears!

رحيل

أصْعَدُ درجَ الورد... على مَداخلِ البيت المهجور، فَتستقبلُني ورودٌ عطشى إلى الماء، وظَمْأى إلى يدٍ كانت تُلامِسُ أوراقها بحنان، وتفْرُشُ تُرابَها بضوءِ العيونِ وحكايا السَّهر!

مِثْلُ هذه الدُّورِ الجميلة... التي أطلعَتْ حدائقُها مواسمَ الأزاهيرِ والعبير، كانت لي بالأمسِ منازلَ صَحْبٍ وأحبَّة... قبلَ أن يستقلُّوا قِطارَ الرَّحيلِ ويُهاجِروا!

كلُّ البيوتِ التي هجَرها أهلُها، حكايتُها كحكايةِ هذا البيت الذي على درجِه العتيق تضيعُ منِّي الخُطى، ومن مُطلاَّتِه المسائية يُبْحِرُ بي شراعُ الذِّكرياتِ!

آهِ... يا درجَ الحنينِ الذي يتسلَّقُ المسافاتِ: إلى غُرْبَةِ مَنْ زرعوا على جَنَباتِهِ عُمْرَ التَّعبِ، ورحلوا من غير جوازِ سفر!

آهِ... كم يُشبِهُ انتظارُكَ حُزْنَ تلكَ العيونِ التي تمُدُّ من أهدابها جسراً للعودة... كلَّما صارَ ليلُ البُعدِ في جُفونها بحيرةً من دُموع!

The Path Of Poetry

Poetry is a risky experience.

And love is a risky experience.

Hence, being one of the poet's fighting tools, the word that lives in the bosom of the poet, has to face its destiny with absolute courage.

Therefore, the poet…, who insists on being the only prince of words and love, must not give full rein to his heartbeats or give his words the choice to confront them…

In both his love and poetry, only the poet constantly tries to choose the weapon that guarantees victory for him, not that which leads to his defeat.

Thus, he spends his life divided between his pen's escapades and his heartbeats, seeking the path of salvation!

Two paths, both fraught with dangers… are the path of poetry and the path of love…!

Who said the word can walk on the blade of its sword separating water from fire… without bearing with it the heart of him whose bosom has been transformed by the stabs of that sword into a forest of wounds!

طريق الشعر

الشِّعرُ تجربةٌ خطرة.
والحبُّ تجربةٌ خطرة.

ومن هنا، كانَ على الكلمةِ التي تسكنُ وجدانَ الشَّاعر، كونها إحدى أدواتهِ المحاربة، أن تواجهَ قدَرها بشجاعةٍ مُطلقة.

ومن هنا، كانَ على الشاعر... الذي يأبى إلَّا أنِ يكونَ وحدَهُ أميرَ الكلمةِ والهوى، أن لا يتركَ لقلبهِ العنانَ في خفقاته، وأن لا يتركَ لكلماتهِ الخيارَ في مُواجهتها،...

وحْدَهُ الشاعرُ في حبِّهِ وفي شعره، يُحاولُ أبداً أن يختار السِّلاحَ الذي يُحقِّقُ لهُ الانتصار... لا ذاك الذي يَكتبُ لهُ الهزيمة.

وهكذا، يُمضي حياتَهُ مُحاصَراً بين شطحاتِ قلَمه وخفقاتِ قلبه، وباحثاً عن طريق خلاصِه!

طريقان كلاهما محفوفٌ بالمخاطرِ.. طريقُ الشِّعر، وطريقُ الحُبّ!...

فَمَنْ قال إنَّ الكلمة، تستطيع العُبورَ على حدِّ سيفِها الفاصل بين الماء والنَّار... دونَ أن تحملَ معها قلبَ مَنْ حوَّلَتْ صدْرَهُ، طعناتُ ذلك السَّيف، إلى غابةٍ من جراح!

A Wound And A Rose

Just as the wound transforms into a rose in poetry books and in paintings, so does a rose transform into a wound in the book of life! So why, O Earth, have you hidden the secrets of this tale?

Yesterday we were children playing on your soil… and with the innocence of children, we loved you, and planted you in our imagination as seasons of freedom and hope.

In our childhood we gave you beautiful, wonderful things!

You were for us the love poem that was engraved on all dates, and the tree of freedom that ornamented all seasons!

But since you stopped being our singing that was distributed in the voices of sparrows, and you became our ambition traveling in the flaps of eagles' wings… you have become, O Earth, in our imagination the lost dream, and in our eyelids the fleeing distance.

How could your ideal maternity foster such a conflict, turning your love into a painful wound in our hearts, after being a rose of hope in our eyes?!

جُرْحٌ ووردة

مثلما يتحوَّلُ الجرحُ إلى وردةٍ، في كُتُبِ الشِّعرِ، ولوحاتِ الرَّسْمْ... تتحوَّلُ الوردةُ إلى جرح في كتاب الحياة! فلماذا خبَّأْتِ – يا أرضُ – أسرارَ هذه الحكاية؟

بالأمسِ كُنَّا أطفالاً نلهو على ترابك... فأحْبَبْناكِ في براءةِ الأطفال.

وزرعناكِ في خيالنا مواسمَ حرِّيةٍ وأمل.

أعطيناكِ في طفولتنا أشياء جميلةً ورائعة!

وكنتِ لنا قصيدةَ الحُبِّ التي نُقِشَتْ على كلِّ المواعيد، وشجرة الحرِّية التي زَيَّنَتْ كلَّ الفُصول!

ويومَ لم تعودي غناءنا المُوزَّعَ في أصواتِ العصافير، وصرتِ طموحَنا المُسافِرَ في خفقِ أجنحةِ النُّسورِ... غَدَوْتِ – يا أرضُ – في خيالنا الحُلْمَ الضّائع، وعلى أجفاننا المسافةَ الهاربة!

فكيف لأمومَتِكِ المُثلى أن ترعى هذا التَّناقض، ليصيرَ حُبُّكِ في قلوبنا جرحاً للألم...

بعدما كان في عيوننا وردةً للأمل؟!

With Light… Upon The Homeland Soil

O my homeland, with your sun as my companion,
I am one of your lovers who have never danced on your ashes in the nights of fire.

O My homeland, with your stars as my ancient boon companions at night,
I am one of your poets who have never wearied of writing on your soil with the light of the eyes and the blood of the heart.

Come, let's forgive all those who once imagined that writing with bullets on your breast will construct your new civilization and forge a path for your desired salvation!

Extend – my homeland – to all of us the hand of tolerance. Take us back to your loving bosom.

Our suitcases are tired of traveling. We are tired of our estrangement away from you and of your estrangement within us.

Come back to us as the dream we drew in our school notebooks and sang as chants in the joy of our festive days… when we were children! Come back to us, O homeland, before those chants get old; before we wish that our beautiful dream had remained a child within us and had not grown up!

بالضَّوْء... على تراب الوطن

أنا يا وطني، وشمسكَ لي رفيقة،
واحدٌ من عشّاقكَ الذين ما رقصوا على رمادِكَ في ليالي النّار.
أنا يا وطني، ونجومُكَ سُمَّارُ ليالِيَّ العتاق،
واحدٌ من شعرائكَ الذين ما تعِبوا من الكتابةِ على ترابكَ بضوءِ العيون ودمِ القلبِ.

فتعالَ نغْفِر معاً لمن توهَّموا في يوم مضى أنّ الكتابةَ على صدركِ بالرَّصاص، هي تأليفٌ لحضارتكَ الجديدة، وطريقٌ لخلاصكَ المنشود!

مُدَّ – يا وطني – لنا جميعاً يدَ التَّسامُح. ورُدَّنا أحبَّةً إلى صدرك.
لقد تعبتْ حقائبُنا من السَّفر. وتعِبْنا من غُرْبَتنا عنكَ، وغُرْبَتِكَ فينا.

فعُدْ إلينا ذلك الحُلْمَ الذي رسمناهُ على دفاتِرنا المدرسيّة، وغنّيناهُ أناشيدَنا في فرحِ الأعياد... يوم كنّا أطفالاً! عُدْ إلينا قبلَ أن تشيخَ، يا وطني، تلك الأناشيد، ونتمنّى لو أنَّ حُلْمَنا الجميلَ ظلَّ فينا طفلاً ولم يكْبَرْ!

Lamps

If you wish the evening to be a golden lake for you, be a poetry lover, so that you may constantly sail in the dream.

If you wish your evening to be a post office for love, dip the quill of your waiting into the inkwell of the night, and inscribe your message on a piece of a blue sky!

If you do not love the sunset, turn your eyes into a sea with calm waves and warm ports of longing. Then close your eyelids that you may constantly travel with the sun in the world of light!

But if you ride the yellowness of the sail at the end of the day… submitting to your chanting evening sorrow, do not go holding a green lamp, a mast, or an anchor…! Such a grey voyage will never take you to coasts where anchorages tempt boats, nor to paths whose night is lit by lamps!

قناديل

إذا أردتَ أن يكون لكَ المساءُ بُحيرةً من ذهب، فكن عاشقَ الشِّعر! لتبقى مبحراً في الحُلمِ.

وإذا شِئتَ أن يكون مساؤك بريداً للحُبِّ، فاغْمِسْ ريشة انتظاركَ في مِحْبَرةِ اللَّيل، واكتُبْ رسالتك على قطعةٍ من سماءٍ زرقاء!

وإذا لم تَكُنْ من عُشَّاق غُروب الشمس، فاجْعَلْ من عينيكَ، لَسَفر أشرعتها، بحراً هادئَ الموجِ ومرافئَ دافئةَ الحنين، ثمَّ أطْبِقْ جُفونكَ لتبقى المُسافرَ معها في عالم الضَّوْء!

أما إذا ركبتَ اصْفرارَ شراع آخر النَّهار... مُستسلماً لحزنكَ المسائيِّ المُغنِّي، فلا تمضي حاملاً معكَ قنديلاً أخضر، أو صاريةً ومرساةً!... لأنّ مثلَ هذه الرِّحلة الرَّمادية، لا تُفْضي بكَ إلى شُطآنٍ تُغري مَراسيها المراكب، ولا إلى دُروبٍ تُضيءُ ليلها قناديل!

Modernism

In the congestion of languages dwelling on our lips, our facial features and our names have been lost.

We have forgotten how poetry was written on our sky-colored pages…!

We no longer remember the dates for which we walked upon the eyelids of the heart, waved the night in our eyes as a wedding party for the stars, and planted the dream in our imagination as swings on whose ropes the sun played on the moon's balcony.

In the congestion of languages which changed even the color of our eyes… words in our notebooks no longer have warmth or fragrance, as though they were flowers carved from stone, that can neither be written nor spoken…! For language had been an inkwell of giving for our creative pens, which was slaughtered on the altar of our modern culture, with the quill of those claiming to be modernists!

حداثة

في زُحامِ اللُغات التي تسكنُ شفاهنا، ضاعتْ ملامحُ وجوهِنا والأسماء.

فنسينا كيف على أوراقنا التي بلونِ زُرْقَةِ السماء كان يُكْتَبُ الشِّعر!...

ولم نَعُدْ نذكرُ كيف المواعيدُ التي مَشَيْناها على أجفان القلب... كانت تغْزِلُ اللَّيل في عُيوننا عُرساً للنُّجوم، وتزرعُ الحُلْمَ في خيالنا أراجيحَ تلْعَبُ على حِبالها الشَّمسُ فوق شُرْفةِ القمر!

في زُحامِ اللُغاتِ التي غيَّرتْ منَّا حتَّى ألوانَ العُيون... لم يَعُدْ للكلمات على دفاترنا دِفْءٌ وطيب، لكأنَّها زَهراتٌ من حَجر.. ولا تُكْتَبُ ولا تقال!... ذلك، لأنَّ اللَّغة التي كانت لأقلامِنا المبدعة، دَواةَ العَطاء، نُحِرَتْ على مَذْبَحِ ثقافتِنا المُعاصِرة، بريشةِ مَنْ يدَّعونَ الحداثة!

Greater Than All Languages

In the lexicon of the language of love,

there are words that light our green lamps… in the darkness of visions, and words in whose calmness the night lowers its curtains on the dreams!

For decades, I have been wandering among the words of this book, which does not resemble other books.

I have been searching in the writings of beautiful pens… but no language has stood with me in the presence of your beauty, nor has a quill painted with its colors a dream such as this one roaming in your eyes. Until now your love is still greater than all languages, and my silence is deeper than all words!

أكبر من كلّ اللغات

في قاموسِ لُغةِ الحُبِّ،
كلماتٌ تُشعِلُ قنديلَنا الأخضر... في عَتْمةِ الرُّؤى، وكلماتٌ في سكونها يُسْدِلُ اللَّيلُ ستائِرَهُ على الأحلام!

ومُنذُ عُقودٍ من الزَّمنِ، وأنا مُرتَحِلُ في مُفرداتِ هذا الكتابِ الذي لا يُشْبِهُ الكُتبَ.

وحتى الآن... لم أعثُرْ على كلمةٍ لها ملامحُ طفولةِ وجْهِك!

وحتى الآن، وأنا أبحثُ في كتاباتِ الأقلامِ الجميلة... فلا لُغةٌ وقفتُ معها في حَرَمِ جمالِك، ولا ريشةٌ رسَمَتْ بألوانها مثل هذا الحُلمِ الذي في عينيكِ يُسافر. وحتى الآن... وحُبُّكِ أكبرُ من كلِّ اللُّغات، وصَمْتي أعمقُ من كلِّ الكلام!

A Rose Inside A Book

When I sit down to blacken a white sheet with my words… my hand transforms into a pigeon that wants to fly, and my pen into a green olive branch!

For I am looking for words formed from alphabets of stars… not written with drops of blood.
If I write about the homeland… it is an oasis of peace and love.

And if I write about man… it is the voice of truth, goodness and beauty, and the procession of giving which leads to creativity!

Because I do not want my country to be a friend of dreams without truth or a companion of freedom without dignity…
I have no choice but to bear it upon my eyelids a triumphant flag, plant my words in its soil, and go!

I will be content if one day it is said: that at the time of tyranny which set the homeland on fire… I hid my country… a rose inside a book!

وردةٌ في كتاب

عندما أجلسُ لأُسَوِّدَ بكلماتي صفحةً بيضاء... تتحوَّلُ يدي إلى حمامة تريدُ أن تطير، وقلَمي إلى غُصنِ زيتونٍ أخضر!

فأنا أبحثُ عن الكلمات التي تُصاغُ بأحرفٍ من نُجوم... لا عن تلك التي تُكْتَبُ بقطراتٍ من الدِّماء.

فإذا كتبتُ عن الوطن... فَهْوَ واحةُ سلامٍ وحُبّ.

وإذا كتبتُ عن الإنسان... فَهْوَ صوتُ الحقِّ والخيرِ والجمال، ومسيرةُ العَطاء التي تنتهي بالإبداع!

ولأنِّي لا أُريدُ بلادي صديقةً للحُلْمِ من دونِ الحقيقة، ولا رفيقةً للحرِّيةِ من دُون الكرامة...

يبقى لي أن أحْمِلَها على جُفوني رايةً مُنتصرةً، وأزرعَ كلماتي في تُرابها وأمْضي!

فَحَسْبِيَ أن يُقالَ عنِّي يوماً:
إنِّي في زمنِ الطُّغيانِ الذي أحرقَ الأوطان بالنّارِ... خبَّأتُ بلادي وردةً في كِتابْ!

Your Eyes And I

I get tired of my dialogue with colors… so I run away from thinking about your distant eyes!

I get tired of sailing in the light of words, so I try to forget your conversations implanted in my memory!

I get bored of waiting under the sun and under the rain, so I banish from my mind the image of the little love diary that accompanied our first dates and our first words…!

But,
despite the lapse of time,
and the curtains of fog lowered on the eyelids of paths and dimensions of imagination,
your eyes are still for me a homeland
to which I travel every day!

أنا وعيناكِ

أتْعَبُ من حِواري مع الألوان... فأهربُ من تفكيري بعيْنَيْكِ البَعيدتين!

أتْعَبُ من الإبحارِ في ضَوْءِ الكلمات، فأُحاولُ أن أنسى أحاديثكِ المزْروعة في ذاكرتي!

وأمَلُ الانتظارَ تحتَ الشَّمْسِ، وتحت المَطر، فأُطْرُدُ من مُخيِّلَتي صورة مُفكِّرةِ الحُبِّ الصَّغيرة رفيقةِ مواعيدِنا الأُولى وكلماتِنا الأُولى!...

ولكنْ،
برغم مُرور الزَّمن،
وانْسِدالِ سَتائِرِ الضَّبابِ على جُفونِ الدُّروبِ وأبعاد الخيالِ،
ما زالت عيناكِ لي وَطناً
إليه في كلِّ يومٍ أُسافِرِ!

Letters From The Age Of Poetry

Long ago,
you wrote me from a city that you then called the city of the sun and freedom…!

You wrote: If only you knew, my friend, how a person changes when they move from poor, simple villages and live in rich, liberal, civilized cities!

And how I wish you shared my conviction that your presence here would be an important step in fulfilling your wishes, which you so often told me about.

I remember that on that day I charged my response to you with all the egotism of the poor village young man… trying to conceal my intense desire to be a resident of that wonderful city.

I do not know if you laughed at me or cried for me… when you read my sentence in which I said: However progressive and civilized that city is, golden chariots of poetry never pass through it; nor is it visited by night fairies who trickle dreams in lovers' eyelids.

It was not long ago that we had this dialogue – my friend – when we had villages that loved reading poetry, and cities that enjoyed writing letters!

رسائل من زمن الشِّعر

مِن زَمان.
كتَبْتِ لي من مدينةٍ سَمَّيْتِها في رسالتِكِ يوْمَذاك، مدينة الشَّمْسِ والحُرِّية!...

كتَبْتِ لي تقولين: لو تعرفُ يا صديقي كم يتَغيَّرُ الإنسانُ بانتقالِهِ من سُكْنى القُرى الفقيرةِ البسيطة، إلى سُكْنى المُدُنِ الغَنيَّةِ المُتحرِّرة، والمُتحضِّرة!

وكم أوَدُّ لو تُشاركني قناعَتي بأنَّ وُجودَكَ هُنا سيُشكِّلُ خُطوةً هامة في سبيلِ تحقيقِ أُمْنياتِكَ التي طالما حدَّدْتِني عَنْها.

وأذكرُ أنَّني يوَمَذاك، حَمَّلْتُ رسالتي الجوابيّة إليكِ كلَّ غُرورِ فتى القرية الفقير... مُحاولاً أن أُخْفي رغبتي الصّارخة في أن أكونَ مُقيماً في تلك المدينةِ الرائعة.

ولا أدري إذا كنتِ قد ضحكْتِ مِنّي، أمْ بكيتِ من أجْلي... حين قَرأْتِ عباراتي التي قلتُ فيها: إنَّ تلكَ المدينة على ما لها من الرُّقيِّ والحضارة، لا تمرُّ بها عرباتُ الشِّعْرِ الذَّهبيَّة، ولا تزورُها جِنِّياتُ اللَّيْلِ اللَّواتي يُقَطِّرْنَ الأحلامَ في جُفونِ العُشَّاق!...

من زمانٍ غير بعيد، كان بيْنَنا هذا الحوارُ - يا صديقتي - يومَ كانتْ لنا قُرىً تَعْشَقُ قراءةَ الشِّعر، ومُدُنٌ تَهوى كتابةَ الرَّسائل!

Man And Earth

All homelands on Earth… still hang on their walls sad slogans.

All heroes on Earth… still hang on their chests badges of courage.

And the whole Earth – in the shadow of man's greed – is still a prisoner of oppression and slavery.

Meanwhile, we, its inhabitants, contend and compete in our claims of making sacrifices for the sake of liberating it and turning it into an oasis of peace…!

Since their creation, man and Earth have been together in this strange harmony engraved in the mirror of time. Nevertheless, in their strange relationship, they have also been in a state of conflict and defiance…!

Therefore, all that history handed down to us, and all that has reached us from the remains of successive civilizations, has not changed anything of this truth until now…!

Here is the Earth, daily threatening humans with revenge, but never taking revenge…! Here is man, daily packing his suitcases for departure, but never departing…!

الإنسان والأرض

كلُّ الأوطان في الأرض... ما زالت تعلِّقُ على جدرانها شعاراتِ الحرِّيّة.

وكلُّ الأبطالِ في الأرض... ما زالوا يعلِّقون على صدورِهم أوسِمة البطولة.

والأرضُ كُلُّها – في ظلِّ أطماعِ الإنسان – ما زالت سجينة القهر والعبودية.

فيما نحنُ، كمُقيمين عليها، نتنافسُ ونتبارى في الإدِّعاءِ بالتَّضحياتِ من أجْلِ تحريرها وجَعْلِها واحةً من سلام...!

وعلى الرَّغْمِ من أنَّ الإنسان والأرضَ – منذُ كانا – يُؤلِّفان هذا التَّآلفَ الغريب المنقوشَ في مرآةِ الزَّمن... فهُما معاً بهذه العلاقةِ الغريبةِ أيضاً يؤلِّفان حالةِ الصِّراعِ والتَّحدِّيات...!

ولذا، فكُلُّ ما نقلَهُ إلينا التَّاريخ، وما وصل إلينا من بقايا الحضارات المُتعاقبة على عُصوره... لمْ يغيِّر حتَّى الآن شيئاً من هذه الحقيقة!...

فها هي الأرض – كلَّ يومٍ – تُهدِّدُ إنسانها بالإنتقام ولا تنتقِمُ!... وها هو الإنسانُ – كلَّ يومٍ – يَحزِمُ حقائبَ رحيله عنها ولا يرحل...!

Words Never To Be Forgotten

The words that come to you in the evening... are woven from the gold of sunset and traveling with the sails of hope. I am trying to build you a homeland of love... whose stones are made from the light of eyes and whose gardens are dates under the moonlight.

It is the homeland that my alphabets bring to you... the homeland of love and peace... a homeland with which I travel towards you bearing its visage and voice, as though my notebooks have become paths leading to it, and my quill has taken the form of a torch to be lit on its festive days!

My dear ones! My comrades in the journey of the singing alphabets! I will never ever lose my way... For you have been on my pages since I began my journey – pages which carry my great dreams... words never to be forgotten!

كلماتٌ ليست للنسيان

الكلماتُ التي تأتيكُم مساءً... مشغُولةً بذَهَبِ المَغيب ومُسافرةً بأشرِعةِ الأمل، أُحاولُ أن أبْني لكم منها وطناً للحُبّ... حجارَتُهُ من ضَوْءِ العيون، وحدائقُهُ المواعيدُ في ضَوْءِ القمر!

هُوَ الوطنُ الذي تحمِلُهُ إليكم حُروفي... وطنُ الحُبّ والسَّلام... وطنٌ أسافرُ به إليكم حاملاً وجْهَهُ وصوتَه، كأنَّما دفاتري صارت إليه الدُّروب، وريشتي أخذَتْ شكل شُعْلةٍ تُضاءُ في أعيادِهِ!

فيا أحبَّائي، ويا رفاقي في رحلةِ الحُروفِ المُغنِّية، لَنْ أُضيِّع إليكم طريقي في يومٍ منَ الأيَّام... لأنَّكم منذُ بدأتُ رحلتي... وأنتم على أوراقي التي تحملُ أحلامي الكبيرة... كلماتٌ لَيْسَتْ للنِّسْيان!

Epilogue

Anwar Salman

About the Author

Anwar Nayef Salman is a distinguished Lebanese modern poet who is considered to be one of the pioneers of Al-Shamiyah [the Levantine] school, a trend in Arabic poetry that focused on the esthetic aspects of the poem, with emphasis on visual and auditory imagery.

Salman was born in Ramlieh, a village in Aley district, in 1938. In 1956 he graduated from The Universal College in Aley. That same year he won Maroun Abboud Award for poetry. He spent the early years of his career working as a teacher. During that period, he made his debut with a poetry collection titled *To Her* (1959). A few years later he worked for an organization specialized in producing music and song recordings as well as cultural and social programs for Lebanese and Arab radio stations. He also dabbled in journalism, becoming the editing manager of *Meshwar* magazine. Afterwards, he was employed by the Lebanese Ministry of Culture and Higher Education as a Cultural Consultant for Cinema, Theater, and Fares.

At the outset of his poetic career, Salman joined the "Thuraya Circle" (the Pleiades), set up in 1956 by a group of Lebanese poets including Edmond Rizk, Michelle Nemeh, George Ghanim, Chauki Abou Chakra, Nour Selman, Georges Chami, Raymond Azar, and Jan Jabour. Salman was also a member of the Lebanese Writers' Union, and in 1997 he became a board member, a position for which he was re-elected for four consecutive terms. Additionally, he served as a member of a committee that supervised the production of lyrical poetry texts in the Lebanon Broadcasting Station, and a member of the Founding

Committee of the Songwriters and Melodists Council in Lebanon.

Many of Salman's poems were set to music and sung by famous Lebanese and Arab singers. His poem, "I Don't Want An Apology" won the prize of "The Most Beautiful Song" at Carthage Festival, Tunisia, 1994; three years later, another poem, "The Beauty of Beauties," received the first prize at Cairo International Festival for Arabic Songs; and in 1999 he was granted the Arab Pioneers' shield for Arabic song poetry in Cairo, sponsored by the League of Arab Countries.

Salman's poetry was anthologized in several poetry collections and anthologies including:

– *Al Babtain Dictionary Of Contemporary Arab Poets : Poets' Biographies*, Foundation of Abdulaziz Saud Al-Babtain Prize for Poetic Creativity, 2006.

– *Lebanese Contemporary Poetry Anthology,* (ديوان الشعر اللبناني المعاصر. مختارت من أعمال 60 شاعراً بدءاً بخمسينات القرن الماضي). Dar Al Farabi by The Lebanese National Commission for UNESCO, et Hamza Aboud, 2008.

On April 20, 2016, the poet passed away in a car accident near his home in Beirut.

Salman's works:

– *To Her* (poetry collection, 1959).

– "I Called Him the Coming King" (a collection of recorded poems, 1986).

– *Colored Cards for An Age with No Festive Days* (a poetry collection, 1995).

– *I Search in Your Eyes for A Homeland* (a poetry collection, 2004).

– "Your Love Is Not My Path to Heaven" (recorded poems accompanied by music, 2004).

– *The Poem Is an Impossible Woman* (a poetry collection, 2008).

– *Mirrors for Runaway Dreams* (a collection of prose poems published posthumously, 2017).

– A large number of Radio programs as well as Radio and TV interviews.

Studies about Anwar Salman:

– Chreih, Mahmoud (2016). "Thuraya Circle (the Pleiades): Years Of Intellectual Radiation," Al-Binaa Newspaper, [documentary article] November 8, 2016).

– Rizk, Edmond and Magames, George (2016), *Halaket, Ath-Thurayya* (Pleiades Circle). The Notre Dame University press.

– *Tribute To Anwar Salman: Studies And Testimonies* [a collection of 48 articles], (2017). Dar Nelson, Beirut, Lebanon.

– Hundreds of articles in newspapers, journals, magazines, and literary websites.

Nizar Sartawi

About the Translator

Nizar Sartawi is a poet, translator, essayist, and columnist. He was born in Sarta, Palestine, in 1951. He is a member of numerous literary and cultural organizations, including the Jordanian Writers Association (Jordan), General Union of Arab Writers (Cairo), Asian and African Writers Union, Poetry Posse (U.S.), Inner Child Press International (U.S.), and Axlepin Publishing (the Philippines). He has participated in poetry readings and international forums and festivals in numerous countries, including Jordan, Palestine, Lebanon, Morocco, Egypt, Kosovo, and India. Sartawi's poems have been translated into many languages, including English, French, German, Italian, Danish, Chinese, Urdu, Hindi, and Tamil, and Persian. His poetry has been anthologized and published in many journals, and newspapers in Arab countries, the U.S., Australia, Indonesia, Bosnia, Kosovo, Italy, India, the Philippines, and Taiwan. Some of his poems have been set to music and sung by Italian musician and singer Fabio Martoglio.

Sartawi has published more than 20 books of poetry and poetry translation. His last poetry collection, *My Shadow*, was published in 2017 by Inner Child Press in the U.S.

For the last seven years, Sartawi has been working on poetry translation from English to Arabic and Arabic to English. This includes his Arabic poetry translation project, "Arab Contemporary Poets Series" in which 13 bilingual books have been published so far. He also has translated poems for a number of contemporary international poets such as, Veronica Golos, Maragaret Saine, Elaine Equi,

William S. Peters, Kalpna Singh-Chitnis, Nathalie Handal, Naomi Shihab Nye, Mario Rigli, Niels Hav, Candice James, Ashok Bhargava, Santiago Villafania, Virginia Jasmin Pasalo, Rosa Jamali, Taro Aizu, Fahredin Shehu, Pande Manojlov, and many others.

Sartawi lives with his family in Amman, Jordan.

Email Address: nizarsartawi@gmail.com

What critics said about Anwar Salman…

"In Arabic lyrical poetry, there is a school called Al-Shamiyah (the Levantine). Among its masters are Buhturi, Deek Al-Jin, and Nizar Qabbani. In this school, Anwar Salman holds a chair."

Joseph Harb
A Lebanese Poet

"For [Anwar Salman], poetry is the graceful, virgin language of the people, which keeps the bridge of convergence between cultures, fields of knowledge, and art. In this sense he is a modern poet par excellence."

Ghassan Matar,
A Lebanese poet

"Anwar Salman has been antiquated in the cask of inspiration, deeply rooted in the Mountain. He has passed through life experiences and constructed buildings out of words… songs that bring delight, and hymns that stir enthusiasm"

Edmond Rizk
A Lebanese poet, journalist, and politician

"This is what Anwar Salman, the son of beauty in poetry and the son of esthetics in expression did: he removed the dust off the language of poetry!"

Henri Zoghaib
A Lebanese poet

[Anwar Salman] ... was never far off from moderate modernism that does not turn against heritage; he rather follows its example, surpasses it, and adds to it. For this reason, we can call him the poet of neo-classicism and one of its great pioneers."

Chawki Bazih
A Lebanese poet

"Anwar Salman…, the poet of elegance and creativity, knew how to move back and forth between love and the homeland. He filled his quiver with the aroma of love, then scented it with the overflow of the inkpot, the downpour of beauty, the parchments of love, the golden whispers, the stones of the homeland, and the pistils of perfume."

Michel Kaadi, PhD
A critic, poet, and college professor

"With his departure, Lebanon has lost a literary figure who has enriched the Lebanese cultural scene with pioneering creative works that bear witness to his distinguished giving in the field of poetry. The works of Anwar Salman will remain forever in the memory of the Lebanese culture."

Raymond Araiji
A Lebanese Minister of Culture.

"Anwar Salman weaved poetry on the loom of his fingers and isolated odium and hatred on the rhythm of his poetry."

Melhem Riachy
A Lebanese writer, researcher, and politician

"Anwar Salman… is one of those [poets] who retained the honesty of poetic essence of his age, and preserved its magnificent existence, generous presence, and noble values."

Wajih Fanous, Phd.
Secretary General, Lebanese Writers Union

"Anwar Salman's poetic summa is the confession of a poet who suffers for his country, Lebanon, and affirms his poetic mission as being the expression of this passion for his country. His are the fears, his are the fervent utopian desires for peace among all human beings.

Margaret Saine, Phd.
An American poet and critic

"I have been driven by a deep affinity within my soul that connected me with Anwar Salman. By reading and translating his poems, I pay tribute to a poet who has inspired me as well millions of poetry lovers."

Nizar Sartawi
A Palestinian poet and translator

Notes

[1] Margaret Saine was born in Germany and lives in Los Angeles, California. After a doctorate in French and Hispanic Literatures from Yale, she taught at Californian universities. She writes poetry and translates other poets. Her books include *Bodyscape, Words of Art, Lit Angels"* [2017] and five haiku chapbooks. She has also published four books of poetry in Germany. Her Italian poems will be published in *Paesaggi che respirano* [Breathing Landscapes]. *Searching for Bridges*, a bilingual edition of her poems in Arabic and English, was prepared by Nizar Sartawi. Her poems have been published in Jordan, Portugal, Spain, France, Albania, India, China, the Philippines and other countries, as well as in journals on the Web.

[2] In the poet's collection, *Colored Cards With No Festive Day* (1995), the original title of "The Blue Expanse" poem was "Ulysses." The poet, however, decided later to change it.

[3] Said Takieddine (1904 – 1960) was a Lebanese playwright.

[4] A mawwal is a traditional type of song in which vowels and syllables are longer than usual. It is popular in Arab countries in the Middle East.

[5] In Arabic, unlike English and other languages, the sun is feminine.

Inner Child Press

Inner Child Press is a Publishing Company Founded and Operated by Writers. Our personal publishing experiences provides us an intimate understanding of the sometimes daunting challenges Writers, New and Seasoned may face in the Business of Publishing and Marketing their Creative "Written Work".

For more Information

Inner Child Press

www.innerchildpress.com

intouch@innerchildpress.com

www.ingramcontent.com/pod-product-compliance
Lightning Source LLC
Chambersburg PA
CBHW071710090426
42738CB00009B/1723